Adaptive Education: Individual Diversity and Learning

Robert Glaser

University of Pittsburgh

Series Editors: William and Carol Rohwer
University of California, Berkeley

Holt, Rinehart and Winston
New York, Chicago, San Francisco, Atlanta,
Montreal, Toronto, London, Sydney, Dallas

To my colleagues at the
Learning Research and Development Center

Library of Congress Cataloging in Publication Data

Glaser, Robert, 1921-
  Adaptive education.

  (Principles of educational psychology series)
  Bibliography: p. 167
  Includes Index.
  1. Individualized instruction.   2. School environ-
ment.   I. Title.
LB1031.G54   371.39′4   76-56081
ISBN 0-03-015291-7

Foreword

The Principles of Educational Psychology Series

The materials used to present educational psychology to teachers should have two dominant characteristics—excellence and adaptability. The *Principles of Educational Psychology Series* aspires to both. It consists of several short books, each devoted to an essential topic in the field. The authors of the books are responsible for their excellence; each author is noted for a command of his or her topic and for a deep conviction of the importance of the topic for teachers. Taken as a whole, the series provides comprehensive coverage of the major topics in educational psychology, but it is by no means a survey, for every topic is illuminated in a distinctive way by the individual approach of each author.

Numerous considerations require that the materials used

for instruction in educational psychology be adaptable. One consideration is that the readership is heterogeneous, including students in pre-service teacher training programs, of whom some have and others have not taken prior work in psychology, as well as professional teachers in in-service programs who have already completed previous courses in educational psychology. The separate booklets in the *Principles of Educational Psychology Series* are intended to be responsive to these differences. The writing is clear and direct, providing easy access for the novice, and the authors' fresh and distinctive viewpoints offer new insights to the more experienced.

Another consideration is that the format of courses in educational psychology varies widely. A course may be designed for pre-service or for in-service programs, for early childhood, elementary, secondary, or comprehensive programs, or to offer special preparation for teaching in urban, suburban, or rural settings. The course may occupy a full academic year, a semester, trimester, quarter, or an even shorter period. A common set of topics may be offered to all students in the course, or the topical coverage may be individualized. The *Principles of Educational Psychology Series* can be adapted to any one of these formats. Since the series consists of separate books, each one treating a single topic, instructors and students can choose to adopt the entire set or selected volumes from it, depending on the length, topical emphasis, and structure of the course.

The need for effective means of training teachers is of increasing urgency. To assist in meeting that need, the intent of the series is to provide materials for presenting educational psychology that are distinctive in approach, excellent in execution, and adaptable in use.

William Rohwer
Carol Rohwer
Series Editors
Berkeley, California
February, 1974

Preface

This book is aimed toward an understanding of how current educational practice can extend its capabilities to respond to the diverse society it serves. I have examined how a wide range of opportunities for learning can be provided and how individual potential can be enhanced by taking advantage of these possibilities.

Quality and equality in education does not mean offering the same program to all, but offering a program which reaches out to every person to maximize intellectual and social growth. An educational system that is adaptive to the individual has three essential ingredients. It provides a variety of alternatives for learning and many goals from which to choose. It attempts to utilize and develop the capabilities that an individual brings to these alternatives and to adjust to the learner's particular talents, strengths, and weaknesses. Also, an adaptive educational environment attempts to strengthen an individual's ability to meet the demands of available educational opportunities and develop the skills necessary for success in the complex world.

Rather than sounding the alarms for reform, in this book I have tried to describe work that should be started toward the accomplishment of these ends. The principles and examples presented to define the concepts of adaptive education are meant to serve as heuristics for exploration of educational practice and the underlying research and development. In presenting this subject, I have tried to avoid sounding technocratic and overly prescriptive. The problems are too complex for singular approaches. The possible solutions discussed must be looked at from many angles and should be regarded as part of a continuing process to improve our schools.

I have been particularly sensitive to extremes in recent writings on educational reform. At one extreme is vacuous generalization that precludes even the beginning of operational definition. The other extreme is an overly dogmatic, extremely literal presentation of rules and procedures for teachers. I have tried to strike a stance between these two—a combination between an understanding of general principles and specific practices. The principles and practices described should be taken both as serious possibilities for practical use, as well as suggestions for stimulating further change.

In Chapter 1, the general problem of adaptive education is introduced. Some historical background is presented that indicates the persistent concerns with individuality in education and the pervasive attempts to assess and adjust to individual differences. In Chapter 2, alternate models of educational environments that adapt in different ways to individual diversity in learning are described. Various present and past educational practices are reviewed in the context of these models, and the adaptive educational environment toward which the book is directed is elaborated. Chapter 3 discusses the psychological concepts underlying present-day school practices and contrasts these with newer trends in psychological knowledge and theory. Chapter 4 begins to operationalize the concepts of adaptive school environments and presents general principles for the design of flexible, learner-centered school programs. Chapter 5, focusing on the elementary school, illustrates how the principles and practices described in the previous chapter might be realized in practice. A classroom organization and management system, a preschool program, and an elementary school reading and science program are discussed—all of which were developed for an adaptive environment. Chapter 6 discusses the interaction between research and practice, particularly emphasizing the professionalization of teaching through increasing involvement and partnership in research and development.

The dedication of this book to my colleagues at the Learning Research and Development Center of the University of Pittsburgh needs to be reiterated here. The Center includes individuals expert in many aspects of education—classroom teachers and administrators, designers and developers of instructional materials and procedures, methodologists in the evaluation of educational change, and behavioral and social scientists. The research studies, practical developments, and dedication of these individuals have contributed to this book. Our work has been supported by many organizations, particularly in recent years, by long-range support from the National Institute of Education and the University of Pittsburgh. My own thinking about the content of this book was assisted by support from the National

Institute of Education and by time spent some years ago at the Center for Advanced Study in the Behavioral Sciences.

A number of individuals have contributed directly to the preparation of this monograph. My gratitude goes to Patricia Stanton for her extraordinary skill in converting my dictations and writings into comprehensible form and for her production of the final manuscript; my thanks to Charles Teggatz for his editing and literature search in early drafts; and to Denise Insogna for help in proofreading. A special debt is owed to Joan Jewell for insightful and thorough editing of the manuscript that improved the final version. William and Carol Rohwer, the series editors for Holt, Rinehart and Winston, provided extensive constructive critique as well as encouragement.

As a psychologist concerned for many years with the relationships between psychological knowledge and educational practice, I have lived through a number of lively and promising possibilities for educational change and for the potential of behavioral science to assist in this change. Many attempts have reflected short-term surges with little permanent effect. At the present time, there appears to be an accumulation of knowledge, experience, and strategy for change that can provide a basis for sustained new developments. My deepest hope is that this book conveys some of these possibilities to educators and researchers in a way that assists them in their work toward educational change.

Robert Glaser
University of Pittsburgh
January 1977

Contents

Chapter 1 Adaptation to Diversity: Background

Leon Jaworski, Ralph Nader, I. F. Stone, Hannah Arendt, Marshall McLuhan, professors of developmental neurobiology, nutrition, factor analysis, psychoanalysis, ethics, values, sociology of knowledge, theoretical and human population genetics, physical and cultural anthropology, race relations, cultural geography, poultry breeding, demography, economics, behavioral genetics, and the authors of *When Prophecy Fails* would all constitute a consciously nonexhaustive list of the kinds of expertise one would have to assemble in order to account for the genetic and environmental diversity in human adaptive behavior and for the reactions to the accounting.

I. I. Gottesman, 1974

A central and persisting problem of our schools resides in the necessity to design and provide environments that adapt to individual diversity. Commitment to the realization of individual potential, equality of opportunity, and social justice demands that the process of education consider individual differences along all the various dimensions in which they are manifested—differences in needs, interests, abilities, talents, and styles of learning and living.

The fundamental educational task is to design settings for education that are flexible and adaptive enough to handle these differences which derive from an individual's cultural milieu and his or her own uniqueness among other human beings. An educational environment that is not capable of adjusting to these differences inhibits the development of individual potential, becomes elitist and selective, is heavily biased toward the mainstream culture, and perpetuates inequality. When awareness of this fact has risen to a conscious level, educational research and suggested reform have focused on attaining the ideal of education adaptive to individual learners. Attempts to achieve this ideal have been made in one way or another and for better or for worse.

In this book, the search for equality of the educational process is continued. A general design for an adaptive educational environment is presented. Past and present attempts to adapt to individual diversity are described and alternate models of educational environments are presented. Suggestions are made about what might be done based on current understanding of effective school practices, the psychology of learning and cognition, and individual differences.

The book begins with a general discussion of individuality in education and the various past and present attempts to assess and adjust to individual differences. Psychological concepts underlying present-day school practices are contrasted with new trends in psychological knowledge and theory, and the implications of these new trends for adaptive instructional practice are discussed. Having provided an historical and conceptual framework, the book then describes general principles for the design of flexible, learner-centered school programs and illustrates how these principles and practices might be realized in the classroom. Classroom settings and various adaptive programs for developing competence in the skills and knowledge of the elementary school are described. The book concludes with a description of the research and development efforts that are currently underway which can contribute to the further development of new educational environments. As a setting for this discussion, teaching as a profession is analyzed in terms of its relation to science and research.

A Parable

John Gardner (1961) has asked the question, "Can we be equal and excellent too?" However, the question that sets the direction for this book is the paraphrase by Cross (1971), "Can we be different and excellent too?" Being different and excellent requires the encouragement of diversity and the development of individual talents to the fullest extent possible in a complex society. The guarantee of equal access to education is not sufficient for achieving this purpose if the educational environment provided is inappropriate for the development of different individual capabilities. A parable, told by Benjamin (1949), helps to define our concerns.

In a tale given to American educators by George H. Reavis, the wild creatures once had a school in the woods. All the animals had to take all the subjects. Swimming, running, jumping, climbing, and flying made up the required curriculum.

This was a school of no nonsense. It was a good, liberal educational institution. It gave broad general training—and instruction— and education too.

Some animals, of course, were better students than others. The squirrel, for example, got straight A's from the first in running, jumping, and climbing. He got a good passing grade, moreover, in swimming. It looked as though he would make Phi Beta Kappa in his junior year, but he had trouble with flying. Not that he was unable to fly. He could fly. He climbed to the top of tree after tree and sailed through the air to neighboring trees with ease. As he modestly observed, he was a flying squirrel by race. The teacher of flying pointed out, however, that the squirrel was always losing altitude in his gliding and insisted that he should take off in the approved fashion from the ground. Indeed, the teacher decided that the taking-off-from-the-ground unit had to be mastered first, as was logical, and so he drilled the squirrel day after day on the take-off.

The flying teacher's practice in this case was in strict accord with the educational philosophy of the school. The teachers recognized that students would necessarily display great variations in their abilities. In the Woods Normal School, as a matter of fact, the teachers had learned a great deal about individual differences and the consequent tremendous ranges in human capacities. They set themselves doggedly, therefore, to the task of reducing these differences as best they might, that sane likenesses, safe unities, and noble conformities might prevail in the woods.

The squirrel tried hard. He tried so hard he got severe Charley horses in both hind legs, and thus crippled he became incapable even of running, jumping, or climbing. He left school a failure, and died soon thereafter of starvation, being unable to gather and store nuts. He was cheerful to the last and was much beloved by his teachers and fellow pupils. He had the highest regard for his alma mater, regretting only the peculiar incapacity which had kept him from passing the course in flying. . . .

Old Man Coyote, who had been studying the development of education in the woods, shrewdly observed, "All these pedagogical characters are going at this business wrong end to. They look at what animals and birds—a lot of animals and birds—do and need to do. Then they put those needs and those doings into formal schoolings and try to make the little pups and cubs and fledglings fit the schoolings. It's haywire, wacky, and will never really work right." .

Tom Gunn's Mule . . . demanded harshly, "If you're so smart, how would you do it?"

"Why, I would turn the whole thing around. . . . These school people start with things that birds and animals do—or even more often what they did some time ago. . . . Then the teachers hammer these doings—or as much of them as they can handle and as they think high-toned enough—into schoolings, courses, curriculums, and subjects. Then they hammer the pups into the schoolings. It's a rough and dopey process . . . they make a lot of cubs and pups and fledglings mean and rough and dopey when they could and should make them good and slick and smart."

"Sure, sure," snorted Tom Gunn's Mule, "but you still haven't told me how you would do it."

"Turn it around," said Old Man Coyote. "Start with the pups. See what the pups do. Then see what the school can do for the pups. Then see what the pups and the school together can do for all the creatures in the woods. Simple—forwards instead of backwards—right end to instead of wrong end to."

"Hey!" shouted Tom Gunn's Mule. "Wait! These teachers . . . have to run those schools. They are practical people. Just how, specifically and precisely, would you tell them to change their schools so as to get their education right end to, as you call it?"

Old Man Coyote patted a yawn with the back of his forepaw. "I lay down general principles. . . . These schoolteachers have got to figure out some of the minor details themselves." (pp. 1–8)

Unlike Old Man Coyote, we *do* get into certain details in this book. Our aim is to avoid the possibility of school systems such as Benjamin's parable describes—systems that operate in a Darwinian framework, requiring that organisms adapt to, and survive in, an inflexible environment. The alternative is that the environment can be changed. If we design only fixed educational environments, then a wide range of background capabilities and talented accomplishments are lost because individuals must rely exclusively on those particular abilities required for survival in the fixed system.

Adaptation to diversity and the development of individual talents cannot occur in schools preoccupied with "correcting deficiencies," and which are structured to preclude children learning at different rates and in different ways. Instead of attempting to fit students into a monolithic, relatively uniform program, educational institutions must be designed to be adaptable and flexible enough to fit diverse students. Quality and equality in education consist not in offering the same program to all, but in maximizing the match between individual abilities and the environments in which teaching and learning take place.

Background

The problem of designing educational environments in order to diversify the individual experiences of the learner has become increasingly intense since the beginning of the twentieth century (cf. Cronbach, 1967). During the late nineteenth and early twentieth centuries in most European countries and in all American states, systems of universal compulsory education were being organized. Drastic changes were imposed on schools when laws were passed compelling all children to attend. Massachusetts passed the first such law in 1852, and by 1918 all states had some kind of compulsory attendance provisions on the statute books. What compulsory education did was to assemble in one place almost the full range and diverse qualities of individuals. And this made it necessary for educators to struggle with this diversity.

At this time, elimination was the dominant mechanism by which the educational system adapted to individual differences. Schooling largely consisted of fixed curricula, with common branches of knowledge that proceeded through academic high school programs and college liberal arts programs. Less successful students and students who were financially unable to continue their education dropped out along the way. This mode of "individualization" currently continues to operate in vestigial, subtle, or more sophisticated forms.

In 1902, John Dewey published his influential essay, "The

Child and the Curriculum," in which he deplored the undue emphasis on curriculum development that produced uniform, nonflexible sequences of instruction that ignored and minimized the child's "individual peculiarities, whims, and experiences" (1902/1964, p. 342). In contrast, Dewey pointed out in his famous dictum that

> the child is the starting-point, the center, and the end. His development, his growth, is the ideal. It alone furnishes the standard. To the growth of the child all studies are subservient; they are instruments valued as they serve the needs of growth. . . . It is he [the child] . . . which determines both the quality and quantity of learning. (pp. 342–343)

Nine years later, in 1911, Edward L. Thorndike published a book entitled *Individuality*, in which he also stressed the importance of considering the individual characteristics of each learner.

> Specialization of instruction for different pupils within one class is needed as well as specialization of the curriculum for different classes. Since human nature does not fall into sharply defined groups, we can literally never be sure of having a dozen pupils who need to be treated exactly alike.
>
> All thought and action will be more reasonable and humane if we look for variety in men and examine each nature in a scientific spirit to learn what it really is, instead of idly judging it by some customary superstition. (p. 51)

As the twentieth century moved on and the mental testing movement leaped into prominence, the discrepancy between the objective of adaptation to individual differences and the prevailing practices in the schools was noted. In 1925, well-known educators of the time assembled their thinking and reports of their efforts to design individualized settings in the Twenty-fourth Yearbook of the National Society for the Study of Education, entitled *Adapting the Schools to Individual Differences*. In that volume, Carleton Washburne again stated the problem:

> The widespread use of intelligence tests and achievement tests during the past few years has made every educator realize forcefully that children vary greatly as individuals and that any one school grade contains children of an astonishingly wide variety of capacity and achievement.
>
> It has become palpably absurd to expect to achieve uniform results from uniform assignments, made to a class of widely differing

individuals. Throughout the educational world there has therefore awakened a desire to find some way of adapting schools to the differing individuals who attend them. This desire has resulted in a variety of experiments. (p. x)

In the mid-1930s, the prominent educator Ben Wood wrote to Dewey:

As I survey the schools more than a quarter of a century after you wrote these sentences [i.e., in "The Child and the Curriculum"], I find that the child is still neither the starting point, nor the center, nor the end of our educational organization. So far as my observation goes, this is true even in the so-called progressive schools to some extent at least, since all of them start with a predetermined curriculum, and most, if not all of them, seek to apply one uniform standard achievement. (Downey, 1965, p. 24)

Dewey replied:

I think I am inclined to agree with you in what you say about so-called progressive schools. They have, it seems to me, gone much further in setting up a general concept of adaptation of the individual than they have in developing methods for finding out about the abilities, needs and interests of the individual. (Downey, 1965, p. 24)

Now, from the perspective of the 1970s, the same sentiments can be expressed. We still appear to be in about the same place —not very much advanced beyond the situation as it was described by these men more than 45 years ago. The general concept of adaptation to individual differences is central to many recent reforms and counterreforms in education, including programmed instruction, the open classroom, compensatory education, concern for equality of educational opportunity and adjustment to cultural differences, and reorganization and redesign of curricula for individualized instruction. However, in the main, the discrepancy between goals and practice continues to exist, and we still seek the educational flexibility that fosters the development of each individual.

Selection and Prediction of Success in a Fixed System

The major and most sustained attempt to adjust to individual differences has come by way of the mental testing movement and the development of the field of psychometrics for measuring individual differences in aptitude, ability, interest, and personality (Tyler, 1976). Using tests, individual differences have been assessed for the purposes of selecting and placing individuals into existing settings for education, training, and work. As we shall see, the measurement of individual differences through tests and other assessment techniques is a necessary condition, but not a sufficient one, for adjusting and adapting educational environments to individuals; other aspects of the educational system must also be considered. This point will be developed by first examining the origins of present school selection practices.

Standardized Aptitude Tests

About 1890, Alfred Binet became interested in studying judgment, attention, and reasoning (Tuddenham, 1962; Wolf, 1973). Being interested in complex mental processes and having not much evidence to go by, he studied a great variety of tests to find out how children differed. Having little preconception of how "bright" and "dull" children differed, he tried all sorts of measures: recall of digits, suggestibility, size of cranium, moral judgment, tactile discrimination, mental addition, graphology, and even palmistry.

Binet's writings show a great deal of concern for the development of tests of separate faculties, such as reasoning, memory, attention, and sensory discrimination. At first, he tried to develop measures that provided the possibilities of differential diagnosis so that instruction could be adapted to these different capabilities, but he abandoned this attempt. After vainly trying to disentangle and separately measure various intellectual functions, Binet decided to test them in general, in their combined functional capacity, without any pretense of measuring the exact contribution of each function to the total product.

Binet's work set the stage for a call in 1904 by the French Minister of Public Education to determine what might be done to ensure the benefits of education to the least capable children in school. A commission decided that children suspected of retardation should be given an examination to certify that they were unable to profit from instruction as given in ordinary schools because of the state of their intelligence. The officials could not trust teachers to make this selection; there was the risk of segregating the able child who was making little effort and the troublemaker because the teacher wished to be rid of them; and there was the teacher's reluctance to identify or to give low ratings to children from good families or to less capable children with pleasant personalities.

Binet defined his idea of intelligence by trial and error. Starting with the observation that some children in school are bright and some are dull, he identified tasks that distinguished those groups and assembled all these tasks into a measure of general ability. The items in Binet's test were selected on the basis of their success in predicting scholastic achievement in the existing educational system. This was the predictive aim toward which the test was directed and for which its items were selected, and was also the basis upon which its overall effectiveness was validated.

The empirical, quantitative characteristics of Binet's work became attractive in the United States. His test was first translated into English in the early 1900s, and standardized mental testing was developed with technical improvements for the selection of recruits in World War I. The tests developed used Binet's general model of item selection, validation, and standardization. The success of these tests in predicting performance led to the development of comparable tests for all levels of education.

The selective system for a relatively fixed program developed strongly in higher education, and the requirements and philosophy which evolved filtered back into secondary and elementary schools. At the turn of the century, colleges were less uniformly selective than they have been during most of the twentieth century. There were more places available than applicants; and different colleges had widely idiosyncratic entrance requirements ranging from minimum knowledge of the three R's to high-level mathematics, knowledge of particular foreign languages such as Greek and Latin, chemistry and physics, and so on. For a secondary school principal, it was difficult to organize a curriculum to prepare students for these different requirements and at the same time meet the needs of those students not going to college.

A response to this problem of articulating secondary and higher education was made by associations of prestigious colleges in the East and Middle West. In an effort to develop some standardization of college entrance examinations, an agency, The College Board, was established as early as 1901 (Schudson, 1972). Initially, the examinations given by the Board were essay examinations in different subject matters that tested command of the content of specific areas of knowledge. However, this soon changed. As Alfred Binet's concept of intelligence testing was interpreted, as standardized mental testing was developed for the selection of U.S. Army recruits, and as the use of standardized tests in education rapidly increased, colleges introduced "mental tests" as part of their admissions program. The correlation between results on these tests of "the capacity to do college work" and college achievement proved to be higher and more consistent than between other entrance examinations or secondary school records and college achievement. As a result, scholastic aptitude tests, like the current SAT (Scholastic Aptitude Test) and ACT (American College Testing Program) examinations, became popular.

Standardized selection tests of ability and aptitude were also increasingly used to make educational decisions at the elementary and secondary school levels. The essential decision process was based on an assessment of abilities that predicted, to some extent, whether students would profit from the relatively fixed curriculum provided. In the elementary schools, decisions were made as to which students should be put in undemanding slow classrooms, which should be put into a brisk academic track to prepare for higher education, and which should be placed in classrooms for which average accomplishment was expected throughout the completion of high school or vocational school. The general educational and social theory behind this selective system was and is that every individual should go as far in the progression from elementary school through secondary and higher education as his or her abilities for handling the given program warrant. Diminishing returns are reached early or later by different individuals, and at certain points, weeding out takes place.

What has been described above represents one aspect of the way in which schools have attempted to adapt to individual differences. The goals of education are relatively fixed (achieving elementary, secondary, and college credentials), and the program of education and methods of instruction are essentially uniform. In this context, selective testing has developed as a major means of adjustment to individuals.

Differential Rates of Learning

Flexibility has been introduced into the context of this relatively fixed educational setting by altering the rate of learning. If it is decided that certain minimal criteria of competence should be attained in various subjects, then individuals can stay in school until they master these essentials. In this variation, instructional adaptation to individual differences is increased by altering the duration of instruction until some criterion of skill and knowledge is attained. This adjustment to individual differences has been widely practiced in various and modified forms.

Some years ago, many schools employed the policy of keeping a child in first grade until he or she could read a primer. A more recent policy is a nongraded primary unit that some children complete in two years and some in three or four. Homogeneous grouping systems in education are based, to some extent, on the premise that the pace of education can be adjusted, with some groups spending time on fundamental skills and others going ahead. Differential homework assignments on which children spend more or less time is an adjustment of this kind. Differences in rate of learning indeed reflect an individual difference of some importance. Especially when instructional procedures are relatively fixed, altering the rate of instruction can be adaptive to the different needs of learners.

Restricted Access to Education

The use of college admission tests for large numbers of students and the pervasion of tests in all aspects of educational practice triggered a major social controversy in the 1920s, well reported by Cremin (1961). A number of pronouncements asserted that the new tests indicated that only a small part of the population had the intelligence to get into college and profit from it, that most children going to school were not prepared to profit from too much schooling, and that only a fixed percentage of the population could be educated to a higher level with any reasonable personal and social benefits.

These attitudes were attacked strongly for their inherent

elitism. A series of articles on the controversy was sponsored by *The New Republic* in 1922 and 1923. One editorial criticized the assertion that the tests indicated only a few could profit from college, and contended that what the nation really needed was better individualized schooling for children of all social and intellectual strata. In another editorial, Walter Lippman pointed out that while tests in general were useful for fitting individuals into their proper places in an educational program, they were not appropriate for classifying people as educable or uneducable, and such use was leading the way to an intellectual caste system. John Dewey also attacked elitist notions and pointed out that the tests were a helpful classificatory device, but that their use beyond classification had reprehensible social overtones:

The IQ, Dewey argued, "is an indication of risks and probabilities. Its practical value lies in the stimulus it gives to more intimate and intensive inquiry into individualized abilities and disabilities." Barring complete imbecility, he continued, even the most limited member of the citizenry had potentialities that could be enhanced by a genuine education for individuality. "Democracy will not be democracy until education makes it its chief concern to release distinctive aptitudes in art, thought and companionship." Insofar as tests assisted this goal, they could serve the cause of progress; insofar as they tended in the name of science to sink individuals into numerical classes, they were essentially antithetical to democratic social policy. (Cremin, 1961, pp. 190–191)*

Among the most progressive and liberal critics of the system, there was a general attack upon restricted access imposed upon education by selective testing; but at the same time, there was the sense that some objective measures were required whereby the educator could be informed about how to educate each individual and hence preserve the democratic idea in education. Since the 1920s, the testing controversy has continued to blow hot and cold, and current debates rage over what tests actually measure and how they should be used for education (Cronbach, 1975). In the meantime, as described below, a more differentiated form of testing to assess individuals for alternative educational programs was developed as a partial response to these concerns and as a means of satisfying the needs of a greatly expanded school population.

* Cremin quoted from John Dewey's article, "Mediocrity and Individuality," *The New Republic,* 1922, **33**, 35–37.

Optional Educational Goals
with Fixed Forms of Instruction

Between 1910 and the end of World War II, the colleges remained the province of the minority, while the high schools were transformed into a system of mass education that began to serve all youngsters. Secondary school enrollment rose between 1910 and 1940 from 1.1 million to 7.1 million students, from 15 percent to more than 70 percent of the high school age population (Schudson, 1972). With this great influx of a broad spectrum of students, a single fixed mode of education was undesirable, and another mode of adapting to individual differences became prevalent in order to make high school curricula appropriate for the greater variety of students in attendance. This mode adapts to individual differences by providing options for different educational goals. Different curriculum options are available, and the student is guided to, or selects, curricula pertinent to a prospective future vocation or major field of study. As this system has mainly operated (some years ago and to a large extent today), students with different goals are channeled into different options such as academic, vocational, or business-oriented courses. Adapting to individual differences in this way requires that the educational system make provision for optional educational goals and objectives, but generally, within each option, the instructional program and techniques of teaching are relatively fixed.

In the early forms of this mode of adaptation, as well as in those of today, the different options offered have varying status implications. The academic curriculum has had higher prestige than the vocational curriculum. In this context, the discipline of mathematics, for example, was offered as part of the academic option, while "business arithmetic" was offered in the less prestigious, vocationally oriented option. This has changed somewhat in today's school, where it is increasingly common to have mathematics courses in each curriculum option so that every pupil gains an understanding of the basic concepts of the discipline. The courses differ, however, in their depth and extensiveness. Less common is the effort to teach certain advanced mathematical competencies to youngsters in all curricula options, using a variety of instructional techniques that are adjusted to individual differences and backgrounds.

Differential Aptitude Tests

The availability of different courses of study for individuals with different goals was seen as a situation in which tests might be useful in selecting particular courses of study; they might be used to predict the different school subjects that a person would learn most easily or for which he or she was most suited. This led to the development of differential aptitude test batteries to assist students and their guidance counselors in making vocational and educational decisions. In addition to providing an overall measure of intelligence and general scholastic aptitude, these more specialized tests were designed to provide measures on a variety of more specific factors such as spatial, mechanical, and abstract reasoning aptitudes. It was assumed that different vocations require different aptitude profiles and that specialized test batteries could predict differential success in school programs leading to different vocations.

The success of differential aptitude test batteries has not been outstanding. Early documentation of this was provided by a large-scale study conducted by Thorndike and Hagen (1959). Thirteen years after applicants for aviation cadet training in the Army Air Force in World War II had taken an extensive battery of aptitude tests, Thorndike and Hagen followed up the applicants' civilian careers. With respect to the prediction of success within an occupation, Thorndike and Hagen wrote:

> As far as we are able to determine from our data, there is no convincing evidence that aptitude tests or biographical information of the type that was available to us can predict degree of success within an occupation insofar as this is represented in the criterion measures that we were able to attain. This would suggest that we should view the long-range prediction of occupational success by aptitude tests with a good deal of skepticism and take a very restrained view as to how much can be accomplished in this direction. (p. 50)

In 1964, McNemar carried out a careful analysis of the validity coefficients of certain widely used, multitest, differential aptitude batteries. He argued from his analysis that "aside from tests of numerical ability having differential value for predicting school grades in math, it seems safe to conclude that the worth of the multitest batteries as differential predictors of achievement in school has not been demonstrated" (p. 875). McNemar further concluded that "it is far from clear that tests of general intelligence have been outmoded by the multitest batteries as the more useful predictors of school achievement" (p. 875). In general, a simple, unweighted combination of tests of verbal reasoning and numerical ability predicted grades as well as, or better than, any other test or combination of more specific ability tests. What was measured by tests of verbal and numerical ability was quite similar to what was measured in tests of general intelligence.

More recent evidence reaffirms McNemar's conclusion. For example, a 1971 technical report of the College Entrance Examination Board points out that there is certainly no reason why the SAT could not include measures from other domains in addition to the verbal and mathematical skills tested, and that research to identify these other domains has been an enduring concern. Yet, in over 40 years of the SAT's existence, no other measures have demonstrated such a broadly useful relationship to the criterion of college achievement (Angoff, 1971).

A reasonable hypothesis advanced to explain the above results is that within each curriculum option, while the content differs, the instructional procedures employed are relatively uniform. The aptitude tests used, having been designed primarily for purposes of selection in a relatively fixed system, do not provide a basis for deciding how instruction might be designed to make the attainment of successful performance more probable. They are not designed to identify particular capabilities and talents that can become the bases for learning. The general scholastic intelligence tests predict success in "typical" instructional conditions. They do not assess the influence of more specific acquired abilities that might be related to success if alternate means of instruction were available.

Exploring Alternatives

Some interesting research regarding student characteristics and success in school has recently begun. For example, a book by Wing and Wallach, *College Admissions and the Psychology of Talent* (1971), describes a study of how decisions are made about who goes to college. In particular, the study considers the characteristics of students who apply to college and how admission decisions are made. Wing and Wallach obtained data on a large number of college applicants. These data included standardized SAT scores; academic achievement in high school (i.e., high school grades); and various outside-of-school pursuits as indicated by awards in science projects, prizes in art, music, and writing, or special social service or employment.

Examination of the workings of an actual admissions committee indicated, as expected, that the committee gave strong emphasis to SAT scores and to high school academic achievement in judging the acceptability of its applicants. A few adjustments were made for admitting students on the basis of high or low socioeconomic status. Less effort was made to recognize "nonacademic" forms of talented attainments—i.e., talents other than those already summarized by general aptitude test scores and secondary grade school achievement. Wing and Wallach wrote:

> We may therefore conclude that actual admissions decisions are governed primarily by a disposition to skim off the cream of the crop with regard to SAT scores and high school grades, while also showing preference for students with a few easily identifiable status characteristics. Our observation is that the actual admissions process fails to grant explicit recognition to a rich diversity of human talents that express themselves in nonacademic ways. (pp. 125–126)

Taking these outside accomplishments into account, Wing and Wallach carried out a simulated admission policy that required candidates to demonstrate certain nonacademic accomplishments as well as academic criteria. Under this simulated policy, the membership of the class admitted to college differed substantially, by some 50 percent to 60 percent, from the class admitted by actual committee practices. Furthermore, the hypothetical new class represented a wide spectrum of specific distinguished contributions from outside the academic sphere.

The fact is, then, that adapting to individual differences by differentiating educational goals and courses of study, as serviceable as it has been, is restrictive. The channeling practices of high schools and the admission practices of our selective universities emphasize general intelligence test scores and school grades. They deemphasize skills and knowledge that are acquired in a variety of fields of human endeavor exhibited outside the classroom and which could be closely related to occupational competence. As a result, strong pressure exists on teachers and school administrators in primary and secondary schools to prepare their students as thoroughly as possible for the college admissions "entrance gate" hurdle.

Within the academic scene, relatively little effort is expended in embracing worthy and important nonacademic talents. If such talents were embraced at all levels of education, then the status quo of present curricula would be challenged. School curriculum designers would need to begin to adjust content and teaching techniques to accommodate and to further develop meritorious, specific, real-world talents and accomplishments that students can bring to bear on their educational pursuits.

A Beginning Definition of Adaptive Education

In principle, there seems to be no reason why educational environments cannot be designed to accommodate to variations in the background, talents, and other requirements of learners. Extension of this attitude helps define the concept of adaptive education. An educational environment that is adaptive to the individual learner assumes different ways of succeeding and many goals available from which to choose. It assumes further that no particular way of succeeding is greatly valued over the other. In the educational environments described in this chapter, it is quite clear that the most valued way of succeeding is within the relatively fixed system provided. However, if an adaptive mode can be designed with emphasis on a wider constellation of human abilities, then success will have to be differently defined, and many more alternative ways of succeeding will have to be appropriately rewarded than is presently the case.

The remainder of this book is aimed toward understanding what adaptive educational environments might be and how they can be designed and built. Our focus is on the elementary school system, although what is described is applicable to all levels of the educational system. We hope to provide a framework into which others can fit the details of their own work and experience. The problems are too complex and too diverse to allow for singular points of view, assertions of the right road to reform, and overly rigid prescriptions. Multiple experiments in the schools must be assessed and the information obtained used for the next round of improvement. Any suggested solution should be looked at from many angles, with consideration of intended and unintended consequences, and it should be regarded as only one step in a process of continuous revision.

Goals of Elementary Education: Preparation for Adolescence

In a discussion oriented primarily toward instructional technique and the methodology of teaching, it is appropriate to indicate the kinds of goals and values of schooling that motivate the discussion. Since no discussion of the methodolgy or practice can be value free, we could be accused of being mindless technicians with implicit values that are never directly expressed. So, while this book does not elaborate on the nature of the goals of elementary schooling, the objectives and values behind our discussion should be presented briefly. The expression of these goals will present some criteria by which to assess the alternatives we propose to the present-day predominant system of elementary schooling. In addition, a statement of goals can provide a means of highlighting the particular strengths, weaknesses, and limitations of the approach and methodologies described in subsequent chapters.

Elementary schooling, as envisioned in this book, serves as an environment that develops behavior patterns prerequisite to the fundamental objectives expressed for youth as they come to adulthood in our society. These objectives have been cogently stated in a report by the Panel on Youth of the President's Science Advisory Committee, entitled *Youth: Transition to Adulthood* (1974). The report is directed to the age span of 14 to 24, the age span chosen as the interval between childhood and adulthood. The way in which elementary schooling can serve as a base for the development and accomplishment of these aims for young men and women is briefly presented.

The report describes two broad classes of objectives to which environments for youth should be addressed. One class is essentially self-centered and concerns the acquisition of skills that expand the personal resources of a young person. The second class of objectives centers on others rather than self, and is concerned with the social maturity that is characteristic of mutually responsible and mutually rewarding involvement with others. It is important that environments for youth address both classes and, as the report states, "not merely the former, as schools have traditionally done" (p. 3).

Self-Centered Objectives

First in the self-centered class are the cognitive and noncognitive skills necessary for occupational opportunities and economic independence. This class of objectives includes fundamental capabilities—the use of language and numbers, verbal and quantitative comprehension, and problem-solving and thinking skills—which are the objectives of elementary education. Early education is responsible for effectively teaching these skills so that they are available to most children as a foundation for their further development as they progress to the learning of higher-level marketable skills.

A second objective consists of developing the capability to effectively manage one's own affairs. Self-direction and self-management are prerequisites to success in the complex adult world. Ironically, the environments—largely school environments—in which youths presently find themselves provide little freedom of choice, and thus offer little experience in self-management and the acceptance of responsibility. Elementary school environments should offer increased opportunities for individual self-management so that this development can begin earlier and then be further encouraged in later life.

A third objective is the development of capabilities as a consumer of the cultural riches of civilization. The store of cultural achievements in art, literature, music, or science, which can be experienced from the standpoint of creator, performer, or appreciator, enriches one's life experiences. Toward this end, the report of the Panel on Youth points out that environments should provide youth with the kind of experience with cultural achievements that will enable and motivate them, as adults, to pursue their tastes in those directions. The downward extension of this objective to the elementary school is obviously important so that children can begin to observe and participate in the cultural activities of the community.

A fourth objective is the development of capabilities for engaging in intense, concentrated involvement in an activity.

The most personally satisfying experiences, as well as the greatest achievements of man, arise from such concentration, not because of external pressure, but from an inner motivation which propels the person and focuses his or her attention. Whether the activity be scholarship, or performance (as in dramatics or athletics), or the creation of physical objects, or still another activity, it is the concentrated involvement itself, rather than the specific content, that is important. (Panel on Youth, 1974, p. 4)

Elementary school environments designed to allow children the opportunity to choose, plan, and carry out their own learning activities can contribute to this important aim.

Other-Centered Objectives

A first objective in the other-centered class of objectives is to provide experience with persons differing in social class, culture, and age. For some young persons, this is accomplished by military service or activities like the Peace Corps; for most, opportunities for a range of these experiences are limited. In the elementary school, easing the rigidity of grade-level boundaries so that children can work with others of different ages, providing more opportunity for individual student-teacher interaction and for children to observe interaction between adults, and effective cultural integration can serve as initial experiences toward this end.

A second objective is the experience of having others dependent upon one's actions. In older children, such experiences serve as important apprenticeship opportunities for prospective obligations as spouse, parent, and citizen. In the elementary school, experiences can be designed to provide early opportunities of this kind—where older children assume responsibility for teaching younger children, and where children have the opportunity to observe older teachers caring for younger teachers, or husband and wife teacher teams caring for each other.

A third objective consists of involvement in interdependent activities directed toward collective goals for which the outcome depends upon coordinated efforts of everyone involved. The provision of opportunities where an individual can serve in the capacity of leader as well as follower contributes toward this end. Conventional group instruction in the elementary school may not provide enough opportunity for students to gain early experiences of this kind.

The report by the Panel on Youth points out that the kind of social maturation described by objectives of the second class (other-centered) is accomplished haphazardly, if at all, in the present environment provided for youth. For children in the elementary school, participation in activities of this kind will be less direct and on a less complex scale than those for young adults. But, for young children in the early grades, the school environment can be designed to provide simple experiences that they can manage and also more complex situations which they can learn to manage through observation of appropriate models provided by older children and adults.

It will be obvious that discussions in this book will focus on the first class of objectives—the acquisition of self-centered personal resources and skills. However, the two classes of objectives are inseparable. Personal skills need to be developed in a context of other-oriented skills. Neither class of learning occurs in isolation. A child learns to help another while working on arithmetic problems, or learns to read by reading to younger children. So, while the focus of this book is on personal competence, there is no intention to neglect the outstanding importance of the skills relating to others. It is comforting to know that this area has been significantly highlighted in the report by the Panel on Youth and that the concerns expressed there will feed back to recommendations for the elementary school. The kinds of school arrangements that are envisioned for the teaching of personal competence—modes of instruction that are responsive to individual diversity—can lead to new structures for elementary education into which the skills of relating to others will receive more attention than may be possible in the prevalent organization of the elementary school.

Summary

For many years, educators have been concerned with the problem of designing settings for education that adjust to individual differences. This chapter examines certain prevalent ways in which past and present educational practice has attempted to do this. One way in which this has been accomplished has been to develop formal and informal selective admission procedures for access to educational environments that provide limited options for instruction toward relatively fixed educational goals. Modification to meet individual needs occurs primarily by sequential selection (weeding out along the way) or, less frequently, by altering the duration of instruction in order to maximize achievement. A second way adapts to individual differences by differentiating educational goals. An outcome of schooling is decided upon for or by each student, and he or she is placed in a curriculum program that prepares for that goal, and presumably for that role in life. Within each curriculum program, the course of instruction and options for learning are essentially similar for all students.

These attempts to adapt to individual differences have been closely tied to the testing movement and to developments in the field of psychometrics. The tests that have been developed are designed to measure abilities that predict scholastic achievement —abilities that are helpful in most school work as it is conducted in prevalent school environments. Consequently, the success of the educational system is enhanced by selecting individuals with the abilities required to succeed in the system.

Adapting to individual differences through such selective means, however, can be restrictive. In more ideal educational environments, a wide range and variety of instructional methods and opportunities for success could be provided. The alternate means of learning required would be adaptive to and in some way matched to knowledge about individuals—their background, talents, interests, and the nature of their past performance. It is toward this ideal that this book is aimed.

Since the focus of this book is the elementary school, this chapter describes what its fundamental objectives might be. However, concern for developing patterns of adaptation to individual diversity is necessary at all levels of education, and different approaches need to be considered. In Chapter 2, various models of educational environments that adapt in different ways to individual diversity are presented, and alternatives are described.

Chapter 2 Patterns of Adaptation

It cannot be overstressed that it is not the purpose of human equality to make everybody alike. Quite the opposite—it is a practical recognition that every individual is different from every other, and that every person is entitled to follow the path of his own choosing. . . .

The two aspects of equality . . . are indispensable: the ability freely to choose the goal of one's life and the direction of one's efforts, and the provision of a variety of environments, and of kinds of upbringing and training, suitable for diverse endowments of different persons.

Theodosius Dobzhansky, 1973

A particular pattern of formal education can be described by the configuration of instructional alternatives provided and procedures by which decisions are made about students—by themselves, their teachers, or their counselors. Some educational systems provide relatively few alternatives for getting through the system, and the primary decision to be made is whether a student is or is not suitable for the relatively fixed program. Other educational systems offer more alternatives by providing for different educational goals or by making available various instructional procedures for the attainment of competence. The combination of available alternatives provided in systems of schooling and the decision-making procedures used to place individuals in these alternatives are the fundamental characteristics by which educational enterprises can be described and analyzed. These characteristics are the foci in our attempt to describe formally in this chapter the ways in which educational environments can adapt to individual diversity.

Five models of educational enterprises are discussed, with particular emphasis on the structure of decisions and alternatives (Glaser, 1976). The various models are represented by flow diagrams that show the questions asked at decision points and the possible resulting outcomes as a student progresses through the school years. When such models are written as flow diagrams, they are only sterile skeletal structures of the educational process; but restriction of the models to certain essentials serves to draw attention to key aspects, which then can be elaborated. Using conventional flow-chart notation, diamond-shaped boxes represent decision questions, and rectangles represent alternative outcomes or the state of an individual at a particular time. Various past and present school practices through which adaptation to individual differences has taken place are described in the context of these models. Although we describe these models separately for the purposes of explication, they are not mutually exclusive and are combined in a variety of ways at different levels of education.

Five Educational Environments

Model One: Selective with Limited Alternatives

Consider the first model in Figure 2.1. Individuals come to an educational setting with particular abilities and talents; we call this the "initial state of competence" (Box A). Through teacher judgment or more formal tests of readiness and scholastic aptitude, the characteristics of this initial state are assessed in B. On the basis of this assessment, a decision is made either to place an individual in the standard educational environment, D, for which particular abilities are demanded, or to designate the individual as a poor learner, C, for whom some special treatment is required or for whom the educational system is inappropriate. For those placed in the standard system provided in D, an assessment of a state of attained competence is made at E at certain designated times, with the resulting consequences available at F and G—repeat or drop out, or award credential of graduation.

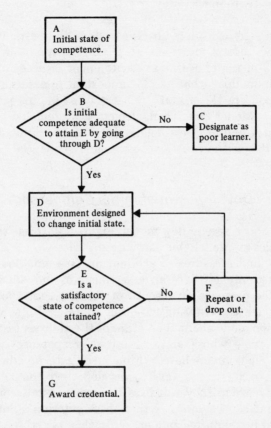

Figure 2.1. Model One: Selective with limited alternatives.

Of course, in practice, this stark model is overlaid with less drastic routines; but for the moment, consider it as given here. The activity carried out in D is generally limited in the alternative modes of learning provided, so the particular abilities assessed, selected, or attended to in B are those individual competencies that are emphasized and fostered in D to the exclusion of other possible abilities.

Thus, at B, there is a monitoring of the abilities required for learning in the environment provided for attaining the competence assessed at E. The success of the system (that is, maximizing the number of students with credentials at G) is realized by admitting those individuals who display at B a relatively high performance in the abilities required to succeed in the given educational environment. Because only those individuals who have a reasonable probability of success in achieving an award at G are seriously considered by the system, the particular educational environment provided at D can be maintained, and little change in the educational environment is necessary. The abilities of individuals that become important to assess and base decisions upon are those that predict success in this particular environment. Model One, then, depicts a system like the one discussed in Chapter 1—a relatively uniform, limited-option program with fixed instructional goals and sequential selection of students.

Model Two: Development of Initial Competence

Consider now a second flow model, Figure 2.2. It has the same characteristics as Model One: an entering gate, an environment for learning, and measures of attainment. At B in Model Two, however, not only is there an assessment of individuals with respect to the presence or absence of abilities that allow them to pass through the entering gate, but there is also some diagnostic decision made about the nature of the abilities tested. For those individuals whose state of initial competence does not allow them to pass immediately through the gate, an educational environment is instituted (H) to develop their competence to the point (I) where they can pass through the gate, or to the point where it can be assumed that these entering abilities will be developed further after gate entry. In this way, through some combination of prior and continued monitoring and instruction, entry gate abilities are modified so that the number of individuals who succeed is maximized.

In practice, one way in which this mode of adaptation operates is by temporarily pulling some students off the mainstream for remedial work. Supplementary instruction is provided to repair a lack of information, a lack of motivation, or gaps in skill. Once they have been brought up to "level," students are returned to the mainstream program. The typical pattern is a major instructional track with side branches in which knowledge and ability required for learning in the mainstream program are provided. For instance, if for some reason or other a child does not have appropriate readiness skills for the options available,

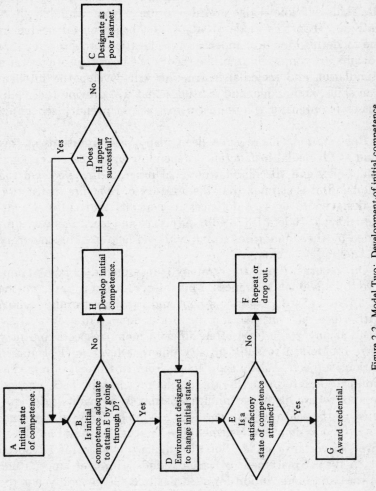

Figure 2.2. Model Two: Development of initial competence.

these skills may need to be taught. In order for a child to profit from the alternatives that are available in reading instruction, it might be necessary to teach some of the basic visual and acoustical process skills that are required for decoding words. If certain self-management skills are necessary for instruction to proceed well in a preschool classroom, these might be taught.

The development of initial competence is a form of adapting to individual differences in circumstances where instructional alternatives are limited and the child must develop the prerequisite skills and knowledge in order to profit from available alternatives. When this mode of adaptation has been advocated in the modern forms of compensatory education proposed for disadvantaged young children, the theory has been that appropriate stimulation and remedial instruction will develop the intellectual skills, knowledge, and attitudes that will provide the readinesses required for the mainstream track of primary schooling.

Remediation. There have been many interpretations of this kind of "remedial instruction," depending upon the educational philosophy and specific instructional program involved. On the one hand, it is claimed that the strategy of remedial instruction is designed to erase differences in personal and cultural individuality; a student is forced to adjust to and learn in a way provided by the standard program, with the help of supplementary instruction if necessary.

On the other hand, the strategy is interpreted as being adaptive to individual differences. This interpretation is based on the fact that individuals enter school and continue through school with quite different learning histories; pupils entering a classroom at any grade level often differ in many respects and may have progressed to substantially different levels of learning in various subjects. When approached from this premise, remediation can be interpreted as the means for allowing each student to start where his or her abilities permit by providing prerequisites in the learning sequence for a subject. Toward this end, some schools do provide elementary, intermediate, and advanced levels of certain courses, and also make provision for advanced or "makeup" placement of various kinds. However, an attitude toward and organization for such flexibility is generally not the norm; rather, it is the exception. For this reason, the situation is best characterized as the existence of a main instructional track, with departures where necessary.

When it is interpreted as remediating "deficits," this mode of adaptation to individual differences has been the subject of serious discussions with respect to education for the "disadvantaged." Debate has centered on connotations of the term *disadvantaged*, when this term is taken to imply a deficit in the learner rather than in the system. In analyzing this term for present purposes, one must look at its operational implications for schooling (including teacher attitudes and differences in classroom climate and school environment).

The deficit point of view appears to be based on the conception that schooling provides a relatively fixed educational track which requires that a learner have certain abilities if he or she is to profit from the instructional opportunities provided. The assumption is that, as a result of a lack of background opportunities prior to the beginning of school, the initial state of competence is lower than necessary to profit from the instruction provided. It is then suggested that some deficit in the learner's competence needs to be remediated so that subsequent instruction can be beneficial.

This perspective emphasizes the view that the deficit or deficiency is in the learner's competence. However, it should be noted that a deficit takes on importance in relation to the particular instructional program provided. If a school provides primarily a nonindividualized, mainstream form of instruction, then a deficit refers to what a child lacks of what is necessary for learning in the context of that particular method of instruction. If, however, a school provides several alternate instructional pathways, then a deficit in one may not be a deficit in another because the prerequisite abilities required in one may be different from those required in another.

The more alternative ways that lead to attaining desired school outcomes, the less outstanding is any one particular deficit or lack of prerequisite knowledge or skill, and the more possible is their adaptation to learners with different entering competencies. This observation suggests that "deficit" can be interpreted in a more constructive way: Rather than using it to overemphasize deficiency in the learner, it can be used to refer also to deficiency with respect to the particular tactics of the instruction provided.

Model Three: Accommodation to Different Styles of Learning

Model Three, shown in Figure 2.3, attempts to respond to the limitations of Model Two by providing alternative flexible instructional environments that accommodate to different learners'

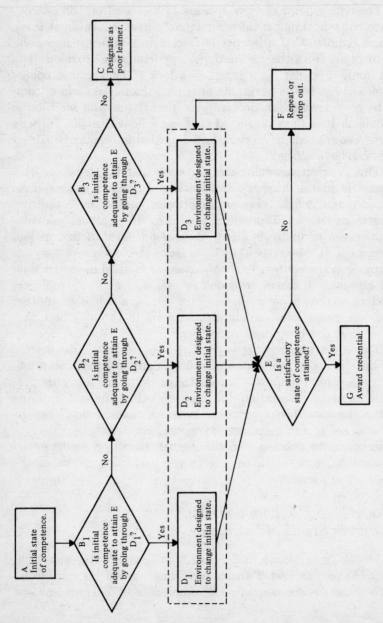

Figure 2.3. Model three: Accommodation to different styles of learning.

abilities. Model Three provides educational alternatives in the form of a variety of educational environments and instructional methods (D_1, D_2, D_3 . . .). In this model, procedures for passing through the entering gate are different from the previous models in which there is only a single path through the system. In the educational setting outlined in Figure 2.3, the attempt is made to match individual abilities to one or more of the environments provided. Individuals who can initially succeed in *any one* of the environments pass through an entering gate. This model assumes that alternative means of instruction are adaptive and are in some way matched to the abilities of different individuals. It may be assumed that this matching process occurs not only at the entering gate, but also continuously during the course of learning. As information is obtained about the learner, decisions are made to enhance probabilities of success in alternate instructional environments with various learning opportunities.

A significant property of this third model is the interaction between a learner's performance and the subsequent nature of the educational setting. An adaptive interaction occurs when there is a match between an individual's abilities and the activities in which he or she engages. The success of the interaction is determined by the extent to which attainment is maximized. This ability-environment matching also takes place in the second model, since the attempt is made there to teach the abilities that enhance attainment in the single, available environment.

In both Models Two and Three, through the pattern of decisions made about individuals and the alternatives available, the institution adapts to individuals rather than, as in Model One, requiring individuals to adjust to the institution. Models Two and Three differ, however, in that Model Two attempts to bring an individual's abilities into a range of competence that enhances his or her potential to profit from the available instructional setting; Model Three attempts to match individuals' abilities to alternate ways of learning, to adapt to individuals by altering instructional procedures.

Altering instructional procedures. One way the third model is realized in practice is the way in which an effective teacher acknowledges and adjusts to the differences among pupils in a classroom by providing alternate instructional paths. Good teachers adapt to individual differences in a great variety of ways. In group or class discussion, the teacher may barely acknowledge the comment of one pupil, but may stop to praise a lesser contribution from a child who the teacher thinks needs special encouragement. When children ask for help from the teacher, the teacher may tell one child that "you can find the answer yourself if you keep at it," but may offer more help to another child. The teacher has decided to encourage independence in the former pupil, but, at the moment, to closely guide and minimize frustration in the latter child. The teacher may require that some pupils do more homework than others, allow some children to teach others, require some children to take a final exam, and offer others the option to do a term paper or develop special projects in accordance with their special abilities and level of competence. A teacher may decide that some students will readily learn on their own, whereas others will comprise the group of students to whom classroom lectures and exercises should be directed.

When teachers act in the ways described above in adapting to individual differences, they are providing different instructional paths and altering instructional methods, except in those cases where they decide that some students just cannot learn, given the time available and the organizational constraints of the class and the school. The teacher functions as a diagnostician by observing students' informal performance and formal test performance, and by picking up cues from other observations. On the basis of this assessment, the teacher makes instructional decisions and alters a student's instructional program on both short-term and long-term bases.

This procedure by which instructional methods are altered for different students is based on the teacher's experience and intuitive expertise. Decisions made in this way are no doubt beneficial to students and adaptive to their requirements. Nevertheless, under various circumstances, these decisions may be inefficient, and at times maladaptive and incorrect for appropriate guidance of student learning and motivation. This is a difficult task, and sometimes students may be "written off" and allowed to just mark time, either because they do not have the prerequisites to work at the level of difficulty of the class, or because the teacher is not prepared to teach at their level.

While this adaptive process depends upon the skills of expert or mediocre teachers and is more or less difficult, depending upon the student population, it is always influenced by the tools, procedures, and organizational flexibility available to the teacher and to the school instructional staff in general. The process can be improved by appropriate diagnostic tests, by the availability of a wide range of instructional situations, and by organizational and technical arrangements for individualizing instruction so that the process of individualization is more adaptive to student differences than is now possible in most schools.

Model Four: Development of Initial Competence and Accommodation to Different Styles of Learning

A fourth model considers the combination of the second and third models; this model is shown in Figure 2.4. In this case, attainment is maximized both by improving abilities required by the entering gate and by providing multiple environments so that abilities and instructional environments can be matched. In any actual realization of the third model, one could only assume a reasonably small set of alternate environments, and the abilities required for these different environments would need to be developed as in the second model. These alternative environments (represented by D_1, D_2, D_3 . . .) refer to a variety of conditions that foster learning and which can be matched to individual requirements.

Alternative environments for learning can be implemented at the present time by changes in school practices; other possibilities can only be dimly envisioned, and await discovery by research on teaching and learning. In no way is an individual fixed in any one track; there can be movement across these alternate environments as the individual develops the skills useful to learn in each context. In practice, Model Four, a combination of Model Two (development of initial competence) and Model Three (accommodation to different learning styles), is necessary for adapting to various individual differences; e.g., slow or fast learners, learning disabled or very bright, and mainstream or minority backgrounds. Consider the cultural variable.

Cultural differences. To ensure the benefits of effective education for all children, adjustment must be made to accommodate the fact that the culture in which young children develop

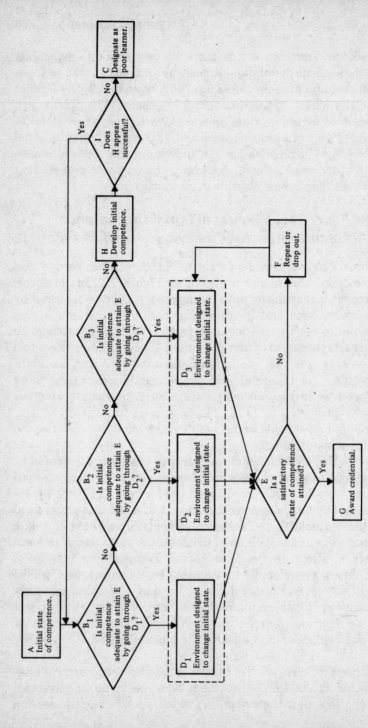

Figure 2.4. Model Four: Development of initial competence and accommodation to different styles of learning.

determines to a significant extent their language, the kind of information they acquire, the techniques they use for processing information, their skills for learning to learn, their themes of interest, and the values and behavioral styles present when they enter and continue in school. When mainstream and minority cultures exist together in a pluralistic society, the demands of a particular school program and the more general school environment may be continuous or discontinuous with the competencies and values that a child brings to school.

"Cultural deprivation" or "being disadvantaged" is then operationally defined in terms of a discontinuity between what the individual and the culture expect of the school and what the school requires. Conventional mainstream schooling, for example, explicitly or implicitly requires immediate acceptance of an achievement ethic with deferred future rewards, a characteristic most consonant with middle-class, mainstream values. For a child coming from a culture with other values, this discontinuity may have a profound effect on the child's behavior toward school and the school's behavior toward the child. In an educational environment that offers options for learning, such values and styles —from whatever source they arise—would be assumed to be competencies of intrinsic worth that have been extremely functional in the child's environment. These competencies can then be treated as the child's assets and can serve as a basis for a program of education.

The disadvantaged perspective can occur only when educational programs are restricted to limited instructional modes that make particular learning styles and initial competencies take on special importance. In contrast, developing the learner's initial competencies to succeed in available instructional programs, as well as providing flexible instructional alternatives, increase the likelihood of success for each child. The attainment of desired school outcomes is more likely because the environment reaches out in many ways to the broad range of competencies in different children.

Model Five: Alternate Attainment Possibilities

Model Five depicts a complex attainment system, in contrast to the simple attainment systems represented by the previous models. A complex model contains different educational outcomes $(E_1, E_2, E_3 \ldots)$, as shown in Figure 2.5. In simple attainment systems, the educational goal is to teach the basic literacies to all students, as is the emphasis of elementary school. Complex attainment systems would be more predominant in higher education. In general, throughout the educational span, complex attainment systems encourage the development of different constellations of human abilities, and can award equally recognized credentials for many different ways of succeeding and attaining different outcomes in the educational system.

Single and multiple attainment systems. The contrast between multiple attainment systems and more singularly focused attainment systems should be elaborated to make clear our concerns for the elementary school. The neglect of possibilities for multiple attainment alternatives in higher education was pointed out some years ago by McClelland (1961). He stressed that if our colleges continue to admit students primarily on the basis of academic merit, as defined by grades and scholastic aptitude tests, everyone will lose in the long run. The colleges will lose because they exclude students who can contribute to making a college experience more realistic and educational for all concerned. Society will lose because young people with very important nonacademic talents—say, strong political talents and mediocre academic ones—will not be exposed to the liberalizing education of college. Most directly, the students lose, both those admitted and those not, because the system tells them that there is only one kind of excellence that counts: the kind of ability that has been described as being fostered by Model One, a kind of scholastic intelligence that results in good grades. According to McClelland:

A single standard of success is being promoted, which, in Riesman's telling phrase, tends to homogenize our cultural value system. Americans all too often, anyway, end up wanting exactly the same thing: the same car, the same standard of living, the same toothpaste, the same wife—all as promoted on television or in the newspapers. Now they must all want the same education—so long as it is the *best* . . . and so long as they can demonstrate what they got out of it, all in exactly the same way, by getting good grades and being promoted upward on the identical ladder of success in the system. (p. 162)

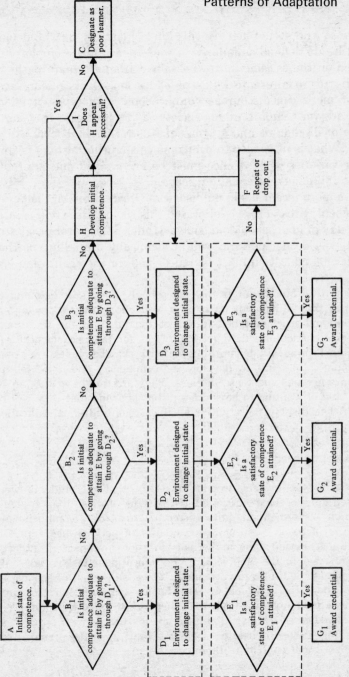

Figure 2.5. Model Five: Alternate attainment possibilities.

Those who do not achieve this kind of success, or who depart from it, are defined as failures in some sense. Little emphasis is placed on the satisfaction to be gained from alternate paths of life based on alternate kinds of education. Overstressing academic merit can discourage young people with types of talent that are very important for society, and can create in them a sense of discontent and a sense of frustration that lasts a lifetime. What is necessary to overcome this crucial mistake is that other varieties of excellence must be encouraged and alternate paths of life must be equally respected.

In a more recent book, published ten years after McClelland's statement, Cross (1971) reiterated this theme. Based on a careful study of high school and college students, she wrote that students who do not perform well academically are telling us that traditional education must be redesigned for the egalitarian era.

They drop out of our traditional schools; they quit listening to lectures; they fail to put forth their best effort; they score low on conventional tests designed to reflect the heart of the traditional academic curriculum; they get low marks for their school performance; their interests, leisure-time activities, and hobbies are "nonacademic"; they fail to develop self-confidence, and they tell us they are nervous and tense in class. They are caught in the impossible bind of wanting to be successful but knowing that they will be required to display the style and values that traditional education will certify. (p. 156)

Cross proposed that

we reverse the present trends to certify that all students were exposed to the same curriculum, certifying instead that students are high performers in quite disparate areas of accomplishment. There must be no compromise on quality of performance, but it is essential to permit wide individual variation in choice of subjects. This reversal in the emphasis of the educational task is not only more humane but also more realistic. Once we get out of school, we choose the areas in which we will display our competencies. Only in school do we require students to display—more or less publicly—their weaknesses. Human dignity demands the right to be good at something. Indeed, a healthy society is built upon the premise that all citizens will contribute their best talents. (p. 164)

The Educational Model of Concern in This Book

It is not unreasonable to equate the selective, limited-alternative features of Model One with certain features of the immediate past and prevailing educational enterprise, as described in Chapter 1. As pointed out, a particular characteristic of such enterprises is that the individual differences that become important to assess and make decisions about are those that predict success in the system. In the environment provided by our prevailing educational system, the present concepts of measured intelligence and aptitude have emerged as the significant entering gate assessments. The history of selection testing in higher and lower education presented in Chapter 1 painted this picture. Binet's work, from which the basic model for scholastic intelligence tests was developed, was especially designed to determine which children were unable to profit from instruction as given in ordinary schooling. College entrance examinations measure certain kinds of achievement and intelligence, and a strong determinant of the nature of primary and secondary education is the character of the entrance requirements to prestigious institutions of higher learning.

This history is to be interpreted in light of the fact that the validation of a test is a very specific procedure; tests are valid for a specific purpose in a specific situation. As a result, the entering gate assessment procedures used in our present educational institutions effectively measure those abilities that contribute to success in the particular environment provided in our schools; these tests predict, to some extent, the outcomes of learning in the limited alternative environment depicted in Model One. They make little or no attempt and are not designed to measure those abilities related to the possibilities inherent in the other models. They are not designed to determine different ways in which students learn best, nor are they designed to diagnose the basic initial competencies that underlie the learning of various kinds of tasks in different environments for learning.

If we analyze the performance requirements of various scholastic settings and then analyze the processes that individuals bring to these task environments, we should be able, in the long run, to match the two and thus change the model of our educational system from the first model to one of the other models. Model Two provides for assistance in the modification of initial competence so that individuals can meet the demands of the learning environments provided. In the third model, individual abilities and styles of learning are matched to various learning environments that utilize these talents. A combination of both these tactics (as in Model Four) appears to be a reasonable way to provide educational environments that are adaptive to individual differences and that maximize educational outcomes.

Analysis of abilities that comprise the initial states of competence upon entrance to an educational system should change the prevalent selective philosophy of Model One to a more adaptive philosophy in which assessments of initial competence are employed to make decisions about what can be done to increase a student's likelihood of school success. The matching of talents and cognitive styles with learning environments must take into account an individual's background and experiences outside of school. Different backgrounds influence specific styles and skills. Adaptive models of education should be able to consider relating such differences in competencies and styles of work to the design of alternative environments for learning.

The basic structure of the educational enterprise that we shall consider as a working framework throughout this book can best be described by Models Four and Five. Since we are primarily concerned with the elementary school's special responsibilities to its students, we aspire toward Model Four as a working goal— amendable as we obtain practical experience and research information—and consider Model Five as a structure that becomes more significant as higher levels of education are reached.

There is a continuum from Model Four to Model Five, a progressive change from single- to multiple-attainment systems. As individuals progress through higher levels of education, they try out their competencies and interests, and develop goals and aspirations in specific areas that can lead to specializations in high school and college. A cyclical phenomenon appears to be involved to the extent that when one enters a particular specialty like reading or mathematics in elementary school, medical school, art school, or electronics training, there is, at the beginning levels, an emphasis on fundamental common attainments and then a move toward further specialization.

Thus, while multiple attainment potentialities are not to be ruled out in the elementary school, we concentrate here on describing single-attainment systems because our objective is to emphasize the necessity of different tactics and strategies of instruction for ensuring that each elementary school child receives the most appropriate education for acquiring the knowledge and skills that comprise fundamental literacies.

The trend toward recognizing a heterogeneity of excellences as individuals progress in their educational pursuits is perhaps an eventual outcome of our vision of adaptive education. However, in primary and elementary education, we suggest that it is necessary to emphasize primarily the basic literacies, skills, and knowledge required by our society. We look upon elementary education in this way: (a) We assume that the primary task of the elementary school is to teach fundamental information and knowledge; certain kinds of skills such as reading, language usage, mathematics, and the techniques of science and art; strategies for thinking, conceptualizing, and problem solving; and attitudes toward people and things. (b) We assume further that it is necessary to design an educational environment that is adaptable enough to enable most elementary students to attain these outcomes or, at the very least, to increase the likelihood that all students will go as far as they can in attaining these knowledges, skills, and attitudes.

The major burden in this enterprise falls upon the act of teaching rather than on the accident of a child's background. It is a matter of shifting attitude and emphasis. The attitude is that most children can learn the skills taught in elementary school, and the emphasis is on providing the proper environment in which this can occur. The question we need to address is: How can education, given a set of particular educational outcomes for elementary school children, be made flexible enough so that the possibilities for attainment are enhanced for all without compromising standards of performance?

It is clear that Model One is too inflexible to accomplish our purpose. It essentially assumes that initial competence is unchangeable and that there is one best way to attain the outcomes of elementary school. Model Two attempts to introduce flexibility, and enhances the likelihood of attainment by recognizing that initial competence can be influenced by the school environment and by instruction. Model Two further recognizes that by not developing initial competence, it is possible for children to build up cumulative deficits which become increasingly crippling—crippling both with respect to the development of competence in prerequisites required for learning the basic literacies for modern living and with respect to long-term attitudinal blockages to the learning process itself. Model Three recognizes that "many roads lead to Rome"; by providing alternate instructional techniques and choices for student self-selection and control, the possibilities for attainment are increased.

As we have indicated, it is Model Four—providing for development of initial competence and accommodation to different ways of learning—that offers maximum adaptability to individual diversity and enhances the likelihood of successful elementary school learning. It is the movement of education toward multiroute patterns of education that is our aim, and we are committed not only to talking about reform, but also to offering operational statements of how to move in that direction.

The new pattern to which we aspire is not all that new. For many years, teachers have been concerned with development of initial competence, especially with respect to the problems of readiness and the sequencing of learning. When we advance the notion of the development of initial competence, we refer to this long-standing concern, and we particularly emphasize that readiness skills and their underlying cognitive structures are greatly influenced by past and present environments in the life of a child. While elementary school teachers frequently adopt the practices of not "pushing" too early and of tending to wait for readiness skills to appear, we emphasize the need to develop more active practices for diagnosing the details of each child's initial competence so that instruction can proceed on a well-informed basis.

Accommodating instruction to different styles of learning also refers, as we have indicated, to the procedures used by good teachers in continuously adjusting their instruction to the progress and styles of the children they teach. This practice needs to be facilitated by decreasing the limitations on the adjustments and alternatives in most present-day classrooms. Procedures and organizational patterns designed for the individualization of learning can produce school environments in which children are taught in different ways in the same classroom. Flexibility is increased by permitting variation in the time required for learning, grouping children from across grade levels on the basis of their level of learning, setting different goals rather than uniform assignments, assigning and selecting different instructional materials and resources, and responding to various patterns of developing interests and talents in the course of learning. The design of contexts and procedures for such flexibility will permit the teacher to make adjustments and the student to make choices to define different paths through the elementary school.

Technical and Organizational Needs

The capability of the schools to adapt to individual differences by altering instructional procedures and programs needs to be further developed. The requirements for this are both technical and organizational in nature. On the technical side, theories of learning and instruction need to make strong contact with school requirements for this purpose. Techniques are being developed for the analysis of how various subject-matter areas can be structured to facilitate learning, of the nature of individual cognitive processes, and of alternate learning strategies that can be incorporated into tools, teaching materials, and instructional practices in order to facilitate instructional flexibility.

Organizationally, the time- and classroom-bound structure of conventional education may not permit the teacher to adjust very readily to different students. There generally is minimal opportunity to consider or devise alternate instructional arrangements that are suitable to the individual progress and idiosyncratic requirements of the children in their classrooms. Even where such arrangements are possible, practical ways of assessing individual differences and procedures for making instructional decisions are not readily available. Some areas are better worked out than others, and teachers are currently offered help in the better-developed areas. Reading and speech specialists, who offer teachers diagnostic services and suggestions for appropriate instructional modification, are available in many schools.

If adaptive education is to become really pervasive, it needs to be studied and integrated into school practice in various forms. The conditions of instruction required for various types of pupils and various types of subject matter must be identified, designed, and evaluated. If this knowledge can then be translated into diagnostic instruments, instructional materials, and new classroom procedures and organizations, then we might come closer to being able to provide the variety of environments required to meet the diversity of human nature.

Summary

Five models of educational environments have been presented, with particular emphasis on the structure of instructional alternatives and decision-making procedures used to place individuals in these alternatives. Our concern is to replace the selective, limited-alternative models with those that are more adaptive to the needs of individual learners. Models that appear to be able to accomplish this purpose have certain general characteristics. They combine the development of an individual's initial competence with the provision of alternate environments matched to different styles of learning. The possibilities for different educational outcomes increase in the progression from elementary school through higher education.

The redesign of schools toward the provision of environments adaptive to individual differences is an obvious requirement on the basis of what appears to be intuitive in good teaching, and detailed study of the performance of expert teachers can help bring this knowledge to others. It is also true that the design of environments for learning should profit from modern knowledge of the psychology of learning and the nature of human development. The more knowledge we have along these lines, the better able we shall be to provide effective instruction. Thus, in addition to the wisdom and practice of good teachers suggesting redirections in the design of educational environments for the elementary school, new developments in psychological knowledge and theory also strongly suggest that change is required. It is to these new developments that we turn in the next chapter before going on to specific aspects of school design.

Chapter 3 Psychology and Education

Old ideas give way slowly; for they are more than abstract logical forms and categories. They are habits, predispositions, deeply engrained attitudes of aversion and preference.

John Dewey, 1909

The present relationship between education and psychology has not been developed through a steady and cumulative process. Rather, it can be viewed more as a relationship which has alternated between progress and regression. There has been, however, explicitly or implicitly, a constant interplay between conceptions of human behavior and educational practice. The psychology of learning and human development has always been a part of teacher-education programs, and beliefs about human behavior that are transmitted to teachers directly or indirectly affect our schools. When one is interested in examining educational practices, the conceptions of learning that underlie them must be analyzed, and new developments in psychological knowledge and theory that can lead to changes in educational practice must be considered.

This chapter examines older and newer psychological notions and their implications for the design of educational environments adaptive to individual differences. When thinking about how psychological conceptions are applied in education, it should be kept in mind that they are not applied with all their theoretical qualifications. The discussion in this chapter is not intended to capture theoretical subtleties; instead, it is intended to highlight the ways in which these conceptions are distilled into educational principles and practices.

At the beginning of this century, education and psychology were closely linked in the work of many psychologists. Individuals like Edward L. Thorndike epitomized the close working relationship between the science of psychology and educational practice. Thorndike (1922, 1923) wrote books for teachers on the psychology of arithmetic and algebra while he was working on laboratory studies of animal learning and intelligence. John Dewey, in his presidential address to the American Psychological Association in 1899, also stressed the importance of the relationship between psychology and education. He said:

> The school practice of to-day has a definite psychological basis. Teachers are already possessed by specific psychological assumptions which control their theory and their practice. The . . . obstacle to the introduction of certain educational reforms is precisely the permeating persistence of the underlying psychological creed. (Dewey, 1900, p. 106)

He went on to say that "in a properly organized system of education," the relationship between psychological theory and educational practice would be the following: "While the psychological theory would guide and illuminate the practice, acting upon the theory would immediately test it, and thus criticize it, bringing about its revision and growth" (p. 120).

In the period following the main work of Thorndike and others like him, education and psychology effectively grew apart. Psychology moved into the laboratory in colleges of arts and sciences, and focused on experimental work and theoretical development. Educational psychology, along with the educational profession, became established in separate schools of education. Over time, barriers of research traditions, special interests, and linguistic conventions demarcated these two areas. As a result of this separation, psychological notions that had been developed in the early contact between psychology and education were distilled and redistilled in textbooks used for teacher education. Only recently, in the past 15 years or so, has the relationship between experimental psychology and educational psychology been seriously renewed.

This separation and reengagement is exemplified by pointing

out that the 1950 yearbook on learning and instruction issued
by the National Society for the Study of Education did not list
in its index major psychologists such an Bandura, Bruner, Hull,
Piaget, Skinner, and Tolman (Henry, 1950). The yearbook
on the same topic in 1964 listed all these psychologists, and
others in abundance (Hilgard, 1964). At the present time, as a
result of a variety of factors—including the general concern for
social change and equality of educational opportunity, and new
developments in psychology—psychologists interested in learning and cognition, developmental psychologists, psychometri-
cians, and social psychologists are restructuring their enterprises
to include the investigation of instructional processes; and they
are receiving more encouragement from the educational profession than in the past. This trend is reflected in the content of
recent textbooks, and is slowly becoming apparent in attempts
to redesign educational environments.

There are various attitudes one can take toward the relationship between psychology and educational practice. One is that
psychology does not know enough to be very helpful in explaining real-world events, and as a discipline, it should work at dis-
covering basic knowledge and at improving theory. A second
attitude is that psychology does have a body of knowledge (e.g.,
empirical studies of the effects of reinforcement, behavior modification techniques, and social learning theory) that is immediately applicable; the need is to train practitioners to properly
use this knowledge. A third is that the application of science to
education is a blight that can destroy the beauty and artistry of
both teaching and learning. Fourth is the attitude that psychological knowledge is not useful in applied settings; innovations
based upon psychological principles have not shown as strong
an effect as, for example, medical practices have in increasing
longevity.

Regardless of the truth or falsity of these assertions, what
does seem indisputable is that commonly held psychological beliefs about the learner and learning are infused into educational
lore by textbooks, dominant educational theories, and professors
of education, and they thereby influence educational practice.
Furthermore, even though conceptions of the learner and learning are changing, the lag time from the expression of these new

ideas to change in practice is very great. The old conceptions may no longer be widely held, but they are fixed in practice. Hence, in order to define new modes of education, it is a useful exercise to match beliefs about the nature of human development and learning with the practices they nurture. Further, it is appropriate to examine the mismatch between educational practice and new developments in our knowledge about learning. To begin this examination, we shall contrast old and prevalent conceptions of the nature of the learner with new thinking. The following contrasts can be made.

1. Older psychological conceptions, which influence current educational practices, have tended to view human beings as having consistent and persistent general drives, dispositions, and traits. In contrast, newer data on ecological and cultural influences require that individuals be viewed as being highly adaptive to surrounding conditions and environmental demands.

2. Investigation of and theorizing about organism-environment interaction has been characterized by a testing of extremes, as exemplified in debates over the relative importance of heredity and environment in learning and development. This focus on extremes has led to serious distortions in educational theory. Current thinking displays a more balanced view of the complex nature and subtleties of the interaction between behavior and environment.

3. The picture of the learner whose predetermined natural development gradually unfolds, encouraged by the work of Gesell and his associates, and the picture of learning through the relatively passive formation of stimulus-response connections, encouraged by Thorndike, have shaped instruction in our schools. In contrast, modern psychology now conceives of the human as an active processor of information and environmental events.

4. The prevalent educational conception of individual differences has been derived from the discipline of psychometrics and standardized testing; this work has emphasized the measurement of individual differences as entities predictive of success in school and work environments. Individual differences in abilities and aptitudes as they relate to education are now being con-

ceived in terms of cognitive processes that can be utilized and developed to facilitate learning and performance.

Each of these four points is further discussed below.

Contrasts in Conceptions of the Learner and of Learning

Constant Traits versus Plasticity and Adaptability

Older conceptions of the learner rested on the beliefs that human beings have consistent and persistent general dispositions or traits, and that their intelligence is an immutable capacity determined by genetic inheritance. People were viewed as having a certain type of personality (e.g., introvert or extrovert) or as having certain personality traits (unsociable, passive, and pessimistic; or sociable, active, and optimistic). These broad underlying dispositions were believed to pervasively influence an individual's behavior and lead to consistency in his or her behavior across many situations. With respect to intelligence, individuals were thought to inherit a general capacity fixed at birth and unaffected by learning. A representative example of this view is provided by Burt, Jones, Miller, and Moodie (1934), who wrote:

By intelligence, the psychologist understands inborn, all-round, intellectual ability. It is inherited, or at least innate, not due to teaching or training; it is intellectual, not emotional or moral, and remains uninfluenced by industry or zeal; it is general, not specific, i.e., it is not limited to any particular kind of work, but enters into all we do or say or think. (pp. 28–29; cited in J. McV. Hunt, 1961, p. 10)

In contrast, newer conceptions emphasize that humans have evolved with a fundamental distinctiveness for trainability, educability, and plasticity of behavior through learning and cognitive growth (Dobzhansky, 1973; J. McV. Hunt, 1961; Lockard, 1971; Mischel, 1973). Recent work in psychology emphasizes the great malleability of humans as a function of learning and diverse environmental conditions, and documents the relatively specific environmental influences upon behavior. Individuals do show generalized, consistent behavior on the basis of which they are frequently characterized as having certain personality traits; but, they are also very good at discriminating and reacting to a variety of situations and experiences in different ways. Older theories of personality err in assuming too much consistency in individual behavior and in deemphasizing the capability of individuals to devise plans and actions depending on the needs, demands, and rules of varying situations (Mischel, 1973).

Roughly the same is true with respect to newer research on intelligence. Even in lower animals, what at one time was called "general animal intelligence" is currently considered to be an aggregate of specific abilities, each of which evolves in response to environmental demands. Animals are "intelligent" in different ways, which can be better understood in relation to the ecological demands of their particular environments rather than in terms of a phyletic ordering according to their general intelligence (Lockard, 1971).

Similarly, the specific capabilities of humans are acquired in the surrounding media of a culture. The capabilities or intelligences developed may be relatively specific to the particular context in which learning occurs. An example of research that demonstrates man's responsiveness to the environmental context is the experimental psycho-anthropological work of Michael Cole and his associates (1971), who studied the cultural context of learning and thinking, using tasks from American experimental laboratories with African Kpelle people from central Liberia as subjects. Through field study and extensive interviewing, Cole observed how the Kpelle people utilize cognitive processes such as concept formation, abstraction, and hypothetical reasoning in their daily activities and social relations. However, Cole found that there was little relation between their use of these processes in their daily lives and their ability to perform the laboratory-designed experimental tasks requiring the use of such processes.

A conclusion of these investigations is that cultural differences in cognitive processes derive more from experience in situations to which particular cognitive processes are applied than from the existence of a process in one cultural group and its absence in another. If this is so, then educational psychology and education should attempt to determine the life conditions under which various processes are manifested, and should then develop procedures that capitalize on and foster these processes to maximize learning in educational settings.

Heredity or Environment versus Organism-Environment Interaction

At one extreme of what has been a polarized debate between heredity and environment (nature and nurture, original and acquired capacities, maturation and learning) is the belief in fixed intelligence and genetically predetermined development. In general, these conceptions assume that an individual's intellectual capacity and related patterns of behavior develop more or less automatically with biological maturation. Both the rate of maturation and the ultimate level of development are viewed as determined by the individual's genetic makeup, and the influence of the environment is deemphasized or neglected (see, e.g., Gesell, 1945, 1946).

At the other extreme is the view that the environment is the primary determinant of the characteristics of the organism. A variety of experiments in which young animals were deprived of sensory experiences or subjected to stress-producing conditions have shown that the rate of maturation is affected by the environment (Riesen, 1965). Experiments with human infants have indicated that the rate of development of certain visual-motor responses can be accelerated by providing them with more stimulating environments (B. L. White, 1969).

Rather than treat heredity and environment as antithetical factors in the development of organisms, newer conceptions view them as having reciprocal and supplementary influences on development. Continuous organism-environment interaction is now seen as a fundamental basis for optimum learning and development. The learner acts upon his environment, changes it, and is in turn influenced by the consequences of his actions. As this interaction occurs, new cognitive structures are developed and new consequences in the environment are set up, which then work together to influence the development of increasingly competent and subtle behavior. The present point of view concerning the contributions of genetic and environmental factors has been concisely stated by McClearn (1969):

There are two essential points which could profitably be incorporated into the *Weltanschaung* of all theorists, researchers, and practitioners in the behavioral sciences. The first pertains to individuality. With the number of [genetic] loci in man estimated to be between ten thousand and one hundred thousand, the possible number of genotypes far exceeds the number of persons now living, plus those who have ever lived, in all of human history. Excepting identical twins, and other identical multiple births, each human being is a unique and unrepeatable event. Add the effects of environment to this genotypic heterogeneity, and individuality is further enhanced. This uniqueness of the individual has implications of the highest importance for both theory and practice. A theoretical formulation which assumes the genetic equivalence of all men . . . is excluding a whole realm of potentially important determinants. . . .

The second point may be stated briefly. . . . We have seen that genotype and environment interact in development. It is inappropriate to view the behavioral repertoire as composed of those traits that are inherited and those that are not. All traits have environmental and genetic components. Thus it is appropriate only to inquire as to the relative proportion of the population variability which is due to differences in genetic and environmental factors. The hoary "nature-nurture controversy" must be replaced by a concept of "nature-nurture collaboration." Understanding of the dynamics of behavior cannot be achieved by ignoring either source of variation. (pp. 32–33)

The Passive versus the Active Learner

Older psychological theories provided a relatively passive picture of memory and mental events that consisted essentially of the acquisition of stimulus-response associations (Ebbinghaus, 1885/1964). The passivity of the learner inherent in this notion led to an emphasis on methods of instruction that stressed rote memorization, with a reliance on repeated exposure to specific stimuli as the basis for acquiring information. Current work in psychology is making it increasingly clear that humans are active processors of environmental events and information; they employ developed strategies to remember and utilize knowledge of events. It is apparent that acquiring information, learning subject-matter skills, and solving problems within the context of a subject matter must be treated as active, constructive cognitive activities.

An example of research that supplies evidence of the dynamic properties of cognitive processes is the work of Bransford and Franks (1971); for another example, see Estes (1974). Participants in an experiment were told a story made up of the following sentences:

The ants were in the kitchen.
The ants in the kitchen ate the jelly.
The ants ate the sweet jelly which was on the table.
The ants ate the sweet jelly.

As these sentences were presented, they were randomly interspersed with other sentences that are not part of the story, such as:

The breeze was warm.
The rock crushed the tiny hut.
The old man read the story in the newspaper.
The hut was at the edge of the woods.

The sentences that formed the story thus had to be extracted and put together from the complete set of presented sentences. After each sentence was presented, the participants were asked to answer a question about it (e.g., "Who?" "Where?"), to be sure that they understood the meaning. After all the sentences were presented, the participants were given a five-minute break, were then presented with the following test sentences, and asked to state whether they recognized any of them as sentences that had been presented before:

(1) The ants ate the jelly.
(2) The ants ate the sweet jelly.
(3) The ants in the kitchen ate the sweet jelly.
(4) The ants in the kitchen ate the sweet jelly which was on the table.

In answer to the question of whether they had seen the sentence before, the participants overwhelmingly chose sentence (4), even though they had not in fact seen it. Sentence (2) was the only one of the four that they had seen, and yet they usually denied having seen it. The participants also usually denied having seen sentence (1), and sentence (3) was second in terms of the number of times that subjects selected it as a sentence that had been presented to them. Looking at the four sentences, notice that sentence (4) most completely expresses the story of the sentences originally presented; sentence (3) less completely expresses that story; and sentences (2) and (1) only partially express it. Thus, the results obtained appear to support the view that not only do individuals "acquire the complete ideas from exposure only to partial ideas, but also that the acquisition of ideas is so natural and compelling that . . . [the participants] would actually think they had heard sentences expressing the complete ideas during acquisition when in fact they had not" (Bransford & Franks, 1971, p. 333).

The active nature of memory as exemplified in this well-known experiment presents a view of the nature of learning that contrasts with classical studies of learning that relied on repeated exposure to specific stimulus-response connections as a basis of acquiring information. Learning and memory is now seen as an integrative process in which there is an active, constructive interaction with events that are encountered in the world. As an individual learns, there is a continual evolution of the structures of knowledge stored in one's memory, and the nature of these structures affects the way in which new information is acquired. Individuals build up different conceptual structures as a result of their different experiences, and hence they can be expected to bring their knowledges to bear upon new learning in different ways. Environmental differences can produce different kinds of memories in individuals, even though the underlying psychological processes for storing, interpreting, and remembering information may be common to all people (see Lindsay & Norman, 1972, chapter 11).

Aptitudes as Predictors versus Aptitudes as Cognitive Processes

The nature of psychological testing and its underlying discipline of psychometrics has led to particular discontinuities between past and current thinking about the way in which individual differences are viewed and measured for the purposes of education. These discontinuities can be seen in terms of two major themes—the notion of psychometric prediction and the notion of aptitude as a fixed characteristic.

The aptitude test tradition has been uniquely oriented toward establishing some measure of an individual's current performance that is predictive of later achievement in the environments for learning generally available in an educational system. In our commonly used aptitude tests, items are chosen primarily for this predictive power. Test scores show that one individual is worse or better than another on some performance that is related to the performance on a criterion task like school grades; so, some purpose is served for selection. Less emphasis is placed upon identifying individual differences in intellectual processes that can be related to the different educational environments that individuals require.

Today, this situation is changing. Psychology has shifted its position to a view that emphasizes the use and development of active cognitive processes, and with this shift has come a change in the attitude toward aptitude. Competent performance is not something only to be predicted; the emphasis now is on how the processes that contribute to it can be influenced. What is being studied is how the individual might be educated to improve his or her cognitive skills to make the attainment of competent performance easier and more effective.

Recent definitions of intelligence and aptitude have stimulated a plethora of research on the effects of instruction on the underlying processes involved. Piagetian theory and cognitive theory in general emphasize matching the child's level of cognitive development with life experiences and are not concerned with differential prediction. Instead, they emphasize developmental changes in processes that influence performance. This view of cognitive processes that are influenced by an individual's learning and development suggests that effective educational practice should be able to identify the differences in individual capabilities to perform these processes. The conditions required to learn school tasks could then be adapted to these differing individual characteristics, or the individual might be taught how to engage more effectively in these processes in order to profit from the kind of learning opportunities provided. At the present time, investigation is being carried out on the extent to which aptitudes and abilities, including the kinds measured on psychological tests, are modifiable and subject to educational influence (Glaser & Resnick, 1972).

Effects of Past Psychological Conceptions on Educational Practice

The preceding brief review of contrasting conceptions of the learner provides a framework for considering how these conceptions relate to educational practice. The overemphasis of the consistency of general traits, and the deemphasis of the adaptivity and plasticity of human behavior, have resulted in the establishment of relatively fixed environments in which education takes place. In essence, once an individual is characterized according to a general potential or disposition, he is placed in the educational setting suited to his nature, and there is little reevaluation of the match between the individual and his environment for learning. This imposed rigidity offers little opportunity for individuals to influence their environment so that it can accommodate their individual requirements. Classroom content limitations and time boundaries make it difficult for an individual not to be victimized by what has been identified as his or her enduring traits and motives.

The overwhelming significance of the nuances of organism-environment interaction has been neglected as a consequence of older psychological theories. The possibilities inherent in the fact that the continuous interaction between individual performance and environmental conditions changes both behavior and the environment cannot be realized in the context of the unyielding environment of most present-day schools. This state of affairs does not provide the flexibility necessary to reach out to the requirements that different individuals have for learning.

The emphasis on the passive organism establishing associative connections and the deemphasis of the human being as an active processor of events have led to the prevalent model of teaching, which is, essentially, the direct transmission of oral or written information from the teacher or a book to the learner. Models of instruction in which teaching is conceived as an enterprise with active construction of information in a problem-solving fashion are relatively less common.

Finally, the usual notion of aptitudes as predictors and not as assessments of current capabilities overemphasizes categorical placement of an individual in a particular educational track and precludes the acceptance of responsibility by the educational system for influencing or adapting to initially assessed performance. This classificatory tactic fails to account for different talents that could enable different individuals to profit optimally from their school experiences.

In general, then, prevalent psychological conceptions of the learner, as filtered through schools of education into school practice, have buttressed the selective, limited-alternative mode of schooling. This prevailing mode of education is characterized, as we have already described, by minimal variation in the conditions under which individuals are expected to learn. A relatively narrow range of instructional options is provided, and a limited number of ways to succeed are available. Consequently, the adaptability of the system to the student is limited to these options, and the availability of alternative paths that can be selected for or by students with different backgrounds and talents is restricted. In such an environment, the available options require particular student abilities, and these particular abilities are emphasized and fostered to the exclusion of other abilities. In this sense, the system becomes selective with respect to individuals who have certain abilities required for success—as success is defined and as it can be attained by the means of the prevailing instructional conditions. Little change in the educational environment is necessary, since only those students who have a reasonable probability of success are effectively admitted into the mainstream of education.

In contrast to the above mode, newer psychological concepts recommend more adaptive educational modes that can provide for a range and variety of instructional methods and opportunities for success. Breaking out of the confines of the selective, limited-alternative mode of schooling requires that we examine contemporary conceptions and their implications for the design of new flexible environments.

Aptitudes as Cognitive Processes: Implications for Educational Practice

One trend that is encouraged by present-day knowledge is a reconceptualization of individual differences in abilities and aptitudes as they relate to education. Abilities and aptitudes need to be expressed in terms of processes that influence learning, development, and performance. The conditions designed for learning can then be adapted to these individual characteristics;

or instruction can be designed so that it directly or indirectly teaches the processes that facilitate learning and development.

What is required is the description and assessment of individual differences in terms of the processes of cognitive performance and demonstrated competence. Individual differences need to be identified in terms of specific kinds of competence and incompetence that enhance and retard learning (Glaser, 1972). Two examples, one at the early elementary school level and the other at the college entrance level, will illustrate how readiness skills and aptitude-related measures can be used as bases for instruction rather than solely as predictors of academic success.

Skills Basic to Beginning Reading and Arithmetic

The first example is concerned with basic processes that contribute to the learning of beginning reading skills. Primary-grade teachers try to consider, and researchers continue to study, the relationships between a child's academic performance and his or her sensory modality preferences. It is commonly believed that some children are visual learners and some are auditory learners, and that instruction is more effective if it takes advantage of this characteristic or aptitude of a child. However, the data on the efficacy of this procedure are not very clear for several reasons. One is that the identification of visual or auditory learners as separate classes of children is not very clear-cut, and techniques for teaching one way or another are frequently difficult to devise in the context of a particular subject matter. A further reason is that in adapting instruction to individual differences, one must consider not only the performance of the child and the nature of instructional alternatives, but also the characteristics of the subject or task being taught. The interaction among these three aspects—subject or task, individual capabilities, and teaching alternatives—determines the nature of adaptive instructional procedures.

Beginning reading, as a task, has certain initial specific demands. The child must learn, among other things, to decode the written language into existing verbal speech, either audibly or silently. Regardless of the instructional program used (phonic, linguistic, or sight reading), the child eventually must learn to associate the letter patterns of language with their corresponding sound patterns. This accomplishment involves at least two critical prerequisite skills: the ability to discriminate between various visually presented letter combinations, and the ability to analyze a spoken word into its component sound parts (a kind of acoustical processing). While the task of discriminating between various visually presented letter combinations is often emphasized, the complicated and demanding auditory analysis task is often neglected.

In teaching children to read, then, a basic question is not whether a child is a visual or auditory learner, but whether he has the visual and auditory analysis skills that appear to be prerequisite to successful achievement. If a child's acquired basic skills include the ability to analyze auditory and acoustical information effectively, he will probably learn to read under a variety of teaching methods. A sight method may be acceptable because the child already brings auditory perceptual skills to the instructional program, through which he can discover the general principles of letter-sound relationships, discriminate the phonetic characteristics of linguistic units, and generate grapheme-phoneme rules. On the other hand, if auditory analysis skills are less developed, the child will be unable to profit very much from sight vocabulary training, will be overwhelmed by any method of instruction that assumes these skills to exist, and will require a program that trains these basic skills.

Consider now the task of learning elementary number concepts in beginning arithmetic. Here, the situation is somewhat analogous to reading in that the child must learn to associate concrete visual information with the symbolic notations that encode them. The child must understand that grouped objects can be identified with quantities and that these groupings can be represented by written symbols, i.e., numerals that indicate how many objects are in a group. A key concept inherent in learning about number concepts and quantity is that groupings and arrangements are indicated by symbols and that the symbols map and represent these arrangements. Hence, elementary arithmetic for a child involves translating the numerals of the problem into concrete visual objects, arranging or combining them, and then recoding the total arrangement back into a numeral. If the child is not able to perform this visual-spatial analysis, he is faced with the problem of learning the numbers by rote and of not understanding their "real meaning."

The absence of well-developed visual analysis skills of this kind may be why certain children require the extensive use of manipulatives. They need to physically construct the groups of objects that are indicated by numerals in order to understand the elementary notions of numbers, sets, and counting. A child who enters a beginning arithmetic program with adequate visual perceptual skills requires less concrete support of this kind. "Seeing mathematical relationships" thus will require support and training for certain children in the basic prerequisite visual perception skills, but will require little or no support or training for children who have already acquired these perceptual skills.

In general, then, a significant readiness skill for beginning reading involves auditory perceptual analysis skills, and a significant readiness requirement for performing primary arithmetic tasks involves skill in spatial perceptual processes. If indeed this is the case, and research strongly indicates that it is (Rosner, 1972), then adaptive educational procedures would seek to determine the strengths of these process skills in children and would attempt to develop them for those children who, for some reason, have not developed them to a satisfactory level of performance—a level of performance necessary to profit from the more advanced instruction.

Verbal Abilities and Memory Processes

Verbal and quantitative abilities are the aptitudes generally measured on tests given to high school students to predict success in college. New research on the nature of these abilities suggests future possibilities for adapting instruction to individual differences. In a series of studies (Hunt, Frost, & Lunneborg, 1973; Hunt, Lunneborg, & Lewis, 1975), students were classified into high and low verbal-ability groups on the basis of a battery of tests used for selection for college entrance at the University of Washington. The individuals in each of these groups were then given a series of tasks employed in laboratory experiments designed to investigate information-processing models of memory. In this way, the characteristics of high verbal-ability students, as defined by aptitude tests, were examined in terms of cognitive processes.

The results of these studies tentatively suggest that there is a relationship between verbal ability and rapidity and efficiency of data information manipulations in short-term memory. In addition to a superior knowledge of language, individuals with high-verbal aptitude displayed certain highly competent cognitive information-processing abilities. They were able to rapidly convert visual patterns of symbols to meaningful letters and words, and to quickly remember the order of these letters and words so that they had more time to concentrate on their meaning.

Since this research suggests that verbal aptitude and ability are related to the rapidity of information processing in memory, the interesting question now is whether we can proceed further and identify situations where speed and other properties of such processing can be taken into account to facilitate school achievement. Perhaps instructional techniques that adapt to slower individual rates of abstracting information from language could be designed to increase long-term retention, or individuals could be given practical exercises to increase their rate of information processing. If such relations between cognitive processes and school success are substantiated, they would have more significant implications than present correlationally derived relationships between entrance tests and school achievement; the process measures would offer clues about how verbal-ability processes might be modified or employed for learning. This would be more adaptive than simply classifying people on the basis of the presence or absence of an aptitude.

Studies such as this one indicate the future promise of a line of research on individual differences which focuses on cognitive processes, and it appears probable that new measures of intelligence and aptitude "will move many psychometric predictions from static statements about the probability of success to dynamic statements about what can be done to increase the likelihood of success" (Hunt, Frost, & Lunneborg, 1973, p. 118). As Hunt and his colleagues further wrote, "Hopefully [this] new viewpoint . . . will lead to measuring instruments which are diagnostic, in the sense that they tell us how the institution should adjust to the person, instead of simply telling us which people already are adjusted to the institution" (1973, p. 120).

By presenting these examples on basic readiness skills in children and on verbal information-processing abilities in adults, we have attempted to illustrate one way in which individual differences must be considered if educational systems are to be more adaptive to individuals than is currently the general case.

The examples cited are only limited illustrations of possible adaptation to individual competence, and the reader may think of others. Obviously, we must also include differences referred to in Chapter 2—differences in skills and cognitive processes that arise from linguistic, cultural, and social backgrounds. The change required is not only that we identify human talents and explicate cognitive processes, but also that we adopt a change of tactic. The old aptitude concept permits primarily measurement of the ability of an individual relative to others, and this measurement provides few clues about educative processes. Hence, little more is suggested than treating people as if they have or do not have an aptitude. In contrast, a new concept of aptitudes that emphasizes performance processes could have less static implications and offer possibilities for educational modifications to increase individual accomplishments.

Design of Adaptive School Environments

In this chapter, some psychological conceptions that have had an impact on educational practice have been briefly sketched. Older conceptions of the nature of human development and learning have in general supported a selective, limited-alternative mode of schooling. In contrast, newer psychological concepts suggest more adaptive educational environments.

An adaptive mode of education assumes that the educational environments can provide for a wide range and variety of instructional methods and opportunities for success. Alternate means of learning are matched to students on the basis of knowledge about each individual's background, talents, interests, and past performance. An individual's abilities and styles are assessed, both upon entrance to and during the course of learning, and educational paths are elected or assigned. Information is obtained about the learner as learning proceeds, and this is used in selecting subsequent alternate learning opportunities. The primary role of the student's current performance in determining the subsequent nature of the educational setting and the constant evaluation of the match between individual performance and the educational environment are the defining characteristics of an adaptive mode.

The success of this adaptive interaction is determined by the extent to which the student does indeed experience some kind of match between his specific abilities and interests and the activities in which he engages. An adaptive school environment attempts to carry out this matching of children's abilities to alternate ways of learning. In the course of accomplishing this, it also attempts to bring the students' abilities into a range of competence that enhances their potential to profit from the available instructional alternatives.

In any form of education, selective or adaptive, the differences between individuals that take on importance are those abilities that have survival value within the system. As a consequence of this, it can be anticipated that in adaptive and interactive educational settings where there is room for adjustment between abilities and modes of learning, wider ranges of abilities can be accommodated, and new capacities can be developed and utilized. What is required is the design of new environments flexible enough to provide the "give and take" necessary to reach out to most learners in order to optimize cognitive growth and the development of competence.

The general task of designing adaptive educational environments is outlined by the following set of questions: (a) How can knowledge of an individual's patterns of abilities be matched to the method, content, and timing of his or her instruction? (b) How can the educational environment be adjusted to an individual's particular talents and particular strengths and weaknesses? (c) How can an individual's abilities be modified and strengthened to meet the prerequisite demands of available means of instruction and available educational opportunities?

In order to answer these questions, one must turn to the practical aspects of education suggested by present conceptions of learning. As has been indicated, conceptions that stress the continuous interaction among individual performance, environmental conditions, and specific environmental influences upon learning and cognition have important implications for the design of adaptive educational environments. The view of individual differences in abilities and aptitudes as malleable processes also has strong implications for educational design. Some general school practices at the elementary school level that are implied by present conceptions of learning and development are described in Chapter 4. This begins the definition of working principles for the design of adaptive educational environments that provides a framework into which educators can fit the details of their own experience.

The technicalities of designing and building flexible educational environments that include the necessary teacher, administrative, and material needs are demanding. But research, development, and implementation toward these ends is what new conceptions of the learner recommend and what is recommended in subsequent chapters. As John Dewey said in his book *Experience and Education* (1938/1973):

> The trouble with traditional education was not that educators took upon themselves the responsibility for providing an environment. The trouble was that they did not consider the other factor in creating an experience; namely, the powers and purposes of those taught. It was assumed that a certain set of conditions was intrinsically desirable, apart from its ability to evoke a certain quality of response in individuals. This lack of mutual adaptation made the process of teaching and learning accidental. Those to whom the provided conditions were suitable managed to learn. Others got on as best they could. (pp. 45–47)

Summary

In keeping with modern psychological theory, the educational environment we aspire to design must emphasize and take advantage of the adaptivity and plasticity of human behavior, rather than rigidly categorize students. Instructional techniques must more fully emphasize the human being as an active constructive interpreter of the events in his or her environment. The school environment must recognize that human beings develop as a function of their interaction with their physical and social environment, and that it is inappropriate to overemphasize either the consistency of original nature or the convenience of uniform and inflexible environments. Further, intelligence and aptitude are now seen as cognitive processess that are subject to instructional influence, and they therefore can become an important subject matter in elementary schooling along with the more traditional subject areas of knowledge and skills. In Chapter 4, we elaborate on some general principles for designing adaptive educational environments that follow from these newer conceptions about human learning and development.

Chapter 4 Principles and Practices

> By 2008 the pattern of . . . education was being
> developed to the point of moving easily and surely
> with the times. It was obviously the greatest factor in
> inaugurating the twenty-first century's great era of
> world peace and progress.
>
> What were the chief characteristics of this new . . .
> education? First, . . . their theory of education
> centered around their belief in individual freedom. . . .
> They believed that every learner was unique, and they
> studied him with care to discover and understand his
> motives, interests, and abilities. In similar fashion, they
> centered their methods of instruction around what
> they knew about the individual learner. . . .
>
> The second main mark of the new . . . education
> was its variety. The primary and upper elementary
> schools were of many kinds, and each of them had
> variety in its own program.
>
> *Harold Benjamin, 1958*

Our discussion so far has focused on general considerations
relevant to the design of educational programs. The task now
is to examine the implications of these ideas so that they can
be realized in practice. To be more than mere advocates of
reform and to be true to our postulates, we must operationalize
the notions that have been expressed and derive principles of
practice from them. Our commitment is to point to how the
structure and practices of elementary schooling can be designed
so that programs are made flexible enough to meet the diverse
needs of students. Quality and equality in elementary school
education does not mean offering the same program to all, but
offering a program which reaches out to every child to maximize

his or her attainment of intellectual, cognitive, and social literacy.

Learner-Centered Education

The key concept underlying the principles for practice discussed in this chapter is that the educational process is essentially controlled by the learner; the child as an individual drives the instructional process. This occurs in two ways: One, the child's distinctive needs, capacities, and abilities are taken into account on an immediate, day-to-day basis by teachers and those planning and conducting educational programs; and two, the classroom environment is designed so that children can make instructional decisions and plan their time and activities for themselves. In these two ways, the educational system flexibly adapts to the individuality of each child and enables children to function as self-generating individuals insofar as their age and experience allow.

Summarized below are some principles or necessary components that underlie learner-centered adaptive educational programs (see Resnick, 1972). In this chapter, these components are presented and then followed by a discussion of the school practices they foster. Chapter 5 gives specific examples of classroom organization and instructional programs that have been developed with these principles in mind.

1. *The human and material resources of the school are flexibly employed to assist in the adaptive process.* The character of resources changes when the shift is made to learner-centered education. Resources need to be more varied and used more flexibly than is currently typical. The conventional boundaries of grade and term levels and the arbitrary time units for subject-matter coverage are adjusted to permit each child to work in the context of his or her particular competencies. Time in a school day is made flexible to accommodate various working styles, and is also used as an asset that children learn to manage. Alternative methods and materials are provided for as wide a range of objectives as possible, and are designed to encompass the interests and backgrounds of the children the school serves. The physical space of the classroom is used in a different way;

space is apportioned in terms of locations for specialized environments where different kinds of learning activities can be undertaken, and where appropriate modes of learning and personal interaction can occur. Teachers, other school personnel, and individuals from the community with various interests, talents, and experiences use their special styles and competencies for different kinds of interaction with children. Increased attention is paid to the particular abilities required by different learning tasks so that the opportunities for matching students and learning activities are maximized.

2. *Curricula are designed to provide realistic sequencing and multiple options for learning.* The structure of the curriculum represents a balance between the extreme of a single track, highly linear sequence with little room for adjustment, and the other extreme of an "open" structureless program in which children choose among activities on the basis of moment-to-moment interest or attraction. For the learner to exercise some control over his or her own learning and for the teacher to have the flexibility required for learner adaptation, the curriculum must have many points of entry, different methods of instruction, various options that lead toward the goal of elementary school competence, and a variety of points at which performance can be assessed. Such a pliable curriculum is, nevertheless, sequenced and structured for instructional purposes. There are sequence requirements that are specified and inherent in the material to be learned, and there are sequence requirements related to the different abilities and knowledge states of the learner. The structural requirements are relevant to future learning and do not consist of unrealistic hurdles.

3. *Open display and access to information and instructional materials are provided.* When various options for learning are available, the problem that arises is the means by which these alternatives are made accessible. For young children in the early grades, the display and access system takes on the form of an environment designed for open browsing. Certain kinds of activities are provided in certain spaces of the school environment. There is a space for reading and language play; there is a space for the investigation of things mathematical; there is a space for quiet work and study on one's assignments; there is a space for intellectual play. The spaces are not rigid and closed

off; they are open and next to one another, and they serve to make visible the available possibilities and the ease with which they can be utilized. There is the opportunity to observe others so that learning by modeling takes place, and there is the opportunity to sample old and new things. The teacher can control the extent of available browsing opportunities when necessary for certain children by asking them to restrict their attention to particular spaces and materials in that space. A significant requirement of the adaptive school is the design of classroom space to encourage the use of available opportunities.

4. *Testing and monitoring procedures are designed to provide information for decision making to teachers and students.* In learner-centered educational systems, tests of various kinds are designed to assist access to particular educational activities on the basis of the student's interests and command of prerequisite competencies. Testing methods provide information for instructional decision making, and these decisions can be made by the learner, by the teacher, or by both together. These tests provide information that informs the learner whether he is making progress toward his objectives and whether he meets prerequisites for some new instructional activity. Testing materials explicitly display the competencies toward which the learner is working.

For effective use in learner-centered educational programs, tests need to become an intrinsic part of the instructional process as sources of information which aid further learning. The function of tests as evaluative instruments to select and compare students is less important. Tests become ways in which the student can assess "how he or she is doing"; they provide the information required to determine next steps or new options. In this sense, a student's performance in the course of learning is frequently assessed and monitored to provide for the effective guidance of learning. Thus, tests frequently are more like workbook exercises that the child and the teacher can examine. So, while test-like events may increase, their character is much different from the usual, formidable evaluative role they generally play in conventional instruction.

5. *Emphasis is placed upon developing abilities in children that assist them in guiding their own learning.* Children are taught the skills that are essential for the effective use of school

resources. They are taught management skills that allow them to assess classroom resources and plan the use of their time. In addition, emphasis is placed on the development of "learning-to-learn" skills—skills that enable individuals to search out and organize information that will be useful to them, and which help them to "program" their own learning so that they can learn more independently of organized formal programs as well as use formal programs more effectively. Children learn to observe the results of their actions, and this feedback helps them modify their future activities. As a result, they learn how to profit from their experience and to consider the effects of their own activity on others and upon themselves.

Furthermore, as psychologists learn more about learning, schools become more receptive to teaching the kind of processes that influence intelligence and aptitudes such as perceptual skills, problem solving, and the ability to remember and use what one remembers for new learning. The teaching of such cognitive abilities can become an expressed part of the curriculum. Management skills and cognitive learning skills in combination produce generative abilities—abilities that give individuals power to direct their own educational experiences, to incorporate new experiences, and to effectively cope with change.

6. *The role of teachers and other school personnel emphasizes the guidance of individual students.* The role of the teacher and other school personnel changes when the shift is made to a learner-centered educational program. Teachers use their particular strengths in different ways. Some teachers are better lecturers than others; some have deeper experiences in certain areas; some are well trained in managing exploratory experiences. Either a single teacher develops a broad range of competencies to accomplish these things, or groups of teachers use their different skills and interests accordingly, openly working with one another. The school may employ paraprofessionals to assist the teachers. In addition, the options that a school has available can be extended by exposing students to people from a wide variety of occupations and community activities that relate to the interests of children—carpenters, artists, news reporters, bankers, construction workers, farmers, and so forth. Nonhuman resources also extend the options of the teacher,

by including computers, movies, TV, radio, and telephone hook-ups that enable students to speak with individuals whose kind of work they have just studied.

Learner-centered education can be implemented in a gradual fashion, and the teacher is, of course, assisted in this by principals and school administrators. Initially, the class may be divided into two or three large groups, which are eventually further divided into smaller groups and individual work as appropriate. Sometimes, a teacher may begin an individualized approach with part of the class and gradually extend it to include the whole class; sometimes, instruction may begin with one subject matter and be extended to other subject matters later on.

Principals and school administrators need to pay attention to the spread and relative progress of students, and to how teachers are deployed to work with the individuals and groups that result. They also need to consider the logistics of supplying materials, including the exchange and redistribution of materials as students in different classes attain various goals and move through the curriculum. Special professional training as well as technical and organizational assistance can be provided to aid teachers and other school personnel in carrying out the management, evaluation, diagnosis, and decision-making functions required for guiding individual performance.

The organization of the school will need to change in order to facilitate adaptive programs. By its nature, the conventional classroom imposes a certain social climate and organizational structure on the school, and most traditional methods of school organization emphasize particular roles for teachers and school administrators. As one thinks about the components described above, questions come to mind. How do these roles and the organizational and social structure of the school change as decision making is shared with the student, as the school takes increased advantage of utilizing options and resources in the community, and as more and more activity is concerned with maintaining a dynamic structure which can adjust to the various achievements of individual children and groups of children? Answers to such questions as these are currently being sought by many school systems (Talmage, 1975).

In the remainder of this chapter, we elaborate on the components of learner-centered programs by considering their practical implications for the classroom environment, the student, and the teacher. Our discussion will center on the use of time, grade level, and grade placement; the characteristics of curriculum materials; the nature of instructional decisions for matching children and instruction; student management of learning; and the role of the teacher.

Time and Grade Level

Time: The Rate and Pace of Learning

The flexible use of time permits teachers and children to use the school day to good advantage in adjusting to individual differences in time preferences and requirements. There are obvious individual differences in this respect: While some students like to spend an extended period of time on their work and complete a task before doing anything else, other children like to work for shorter periods, with some distractions, before completing their work. After finishing a task, some like to engage in some unstructured exploratory activity in order to test and display newly learned skills, while others prefer to reward themselves with some playful activity or with a new subject matter. A flexible use of time can accommodate these differences in preferences.

It also can accommodate children with different styles, such as the impulsive student who responds too quickly, discovers that he has not mastered the exercise, and must go back and review it more carefully; or the reflective student who prefers to be more methodical and to go slowly before testing his learning. Different children also need different amounts of time to comprehend or to practice new materials in order to attain similar levels of performance. Some learn more slowly than others because of previous experience, the necessity for more specific examples, and so on. Maintaining fixed, uniform periods for learning and instruction restricts and penalizes both fast and slow students. Given opportunities for flexibility, different amounts of time can be spent on different subject-matter areas, depending upon the progress and excitement of the child. A skillful teacher can use time in different ways for the benefit of different children, and children can learn to effectively manage their own use of time.

The effective utilization of time is a learned skill that is influenced by environmental requirements. Children learn to use their time more efficiently if they are so taught; they can learn to be responsive to externally imposed or self-imposed deadlines. Given the opportunity for scheduling their time in school, both young and old children can learn to be competent self-managers and, together with their teachers, can greatly assist in the individualization process.

In general, creative use of time may take place through differential assignments to students, self-scheduling by students, and variation in the number of periods in a school day or week that a child uses for different activities. Thinking about time in terms of the individual child, and not consistently in terms of the use of time by an entire classroom group, helps all children to attain the school's criteria for subject-matter competence and to learn the important skill of personal self-management.

Consideration of the adjustable use of time opens up interesting possibilities: Can the school week be adjusted so that students are rewarded and further motivated by days when they are primarily concerned with the exploratory use of what they have learned—through teaching others, through using their new abilities in community projects, and through using their knowledge for problem solving and for other real-life involvements? Can time be found for the teaching of things we do not generally find time for when we have rigid time requirements for scheduling the three R's—time to develop capabilities for and habits of questioning, exploring, and engaging in focused, concentrated activity? Can the time of learning be extended by an extra month of school for some children, and can other children be given the option of spending less time in formal schooling? Can the year-round use of school facilities be encouraged by different time arrangements? Can the special problems of mobile families and children of parents from migrant populations be adequately accommodated?

The Concept of Grade Level

Related to use of time is the concept of grade level and grade placement. The conventional concept of grade involves the annual transition of a student from first grade to second grade to third grade, and so on. The content to be covered each term is fixed by the school system, by the teachers' lesson plans, and by the instructional materials and standardized tests provided for each grade level. It is also constrained by the teachers' experiences, which are frequently restricted to the material and content coverage usually assigned as the objectives for the grade level they teach. A further constraint is the fact that upon entering a new grade at the beginning of a year, some children may have mastered, while others lack, certain prerequisites that can ensure effective learning of the new material. As a result of these restrictions, the conventional class structure is so finely tuned to students in the middle range that it cannot respond to every child. In this sense, a rigid grade-level concept sets boundaries, and limits adaptation of the system to the varying individual requirements.

It is for these reasons, among others, that educators have considered the nongraded elementary school as a way of breaking down the constraints placed upon individual learning by the grade-level structure. The flexibility provided can work to the advantage of the student. Necessary prerequisites can be attended to, children can spend time gaining additional experiences at a certain level of competence so as to move to advanced topics readily; children can relate to one another on the basis of peer tutoring and other experiences; and, overall, the teacher can more closely adjust instruction to the achievement level and needs of each child. While a particular classroom may be kept together to develop important group ties, instruction focuses on children—not as third-grade students only, but as individuals with certain patterns of achievement along a continuum of developing knowledge and skills.

As with most of the general practices we are discussing here, the concept of the nongraded school can be pushed too far. Both the extreme of rigid grade grouping and the extreme of chaotic individualization can have undesirable effects, as teachers know. With appropriate balance and guidance by considered judgments of the child and the teacher, however, adaptive instruction can proceed in a beneficial and manageable way. One practical solution that teachers have found is to consider kindergarten through third grade as one level and fourth through sixth grade as another. Within these units, grade boundaries can be eliminated and, at the same time, movement between the third and fourth grades can be maintained as seems desirable. Student movement through school is then more winding and less linear than is the case in the conventional grade structure, and is guided by teachers who can control the course of learning so that every child is challenged and motivated by a sense of success.

The flexible use of time and a changed attitude toward grade boundaries open the way toward relaxing some of the organizational constraints that militate against adaptive education. The increased opportunity for flexibility, however, requires the introduction of new techniques and procedures to ensure that this new adaptability is manageable and effective; it is to these considerations that we now turn.

Modular Curriculum Materials

The curriculum materials available to the teacher and the child have a significant influence on classroom flexibility. An adaptive environment requires curriculum material that is highly modular; there should be many distinct, separable components rather than monolithic, linear sequences that permit little opportunity for extension and exploration off the main track. Modular materials with varied points of entry, several means of access, and explicit relationships to what the students have already learned, what they should practice, and what they are interested in can provide necessary options in the course of learning. With modular curriculum materials, students can move ahead rapidly if they choose, skip certain aspects, easily go back to certain items when necessary, explore available opportunities for additional perspective and additional depth of information, and take advantage of different approaches to learning. Chapter 5 describes some curriculum programs of this kind.

Accessibility

In order for modular curriculum materials to be appropriately utilized, possible alternatives must be clearly displayed and materials made easily accessible. The difficulties encountered in displaying the possible alternatives vary with the literacy of the user and with the nature of the instructional options and materials. For children who can read, and for use by teachers, written descriptions can convey the option. The task of making the available options accessible then lies in adequately characterizing and cross-referencing the materials. This cross-referencing can involve keying instructional alternatives to measures of performance and accomplishment based on tests and teacher judgments and to the interests of the school children.

Young children who cannot read or interpret lists of choices, and who have a limited range of prior learning experience on which to base judgments of the alternatives, can be provided the opportunity to directly sample various options by an open stack or browsing arrangement where various alternatives may be seen and handled. Browsing and sampling among options can be encouraged by combining physical display of the learning materials with modeling of their use by teachers or more experienced children. The materials are then open and accessible, and children may watch each other at work and thus learn what possibilities are available for future activities of their own. The teacher can guide access to the materials, for example, directing children to various areas of the classroom containing certain kinds of materials or by suggesting that they work only on materials contained in boxes of certain colors or with certain identifying symbols.

Sequence and Structure

For the purposes of instruction, the sequential structure of a subject matter needs to be made apparent so that this structure can be used to facilitate learning and teaching. While all subject matters and skills may not be as organized and cumulative as the early levels of beginning reading or mathematical and scientific concepts, there generally is some inherent structure in a body of knowledge that suggests that certain kinds of information and component skill processes will facilitate the learning of more advanced skills. Fundamental concepts in a subject-matter area are frequently best learned in a relatively structured way; they then provide a basis upon which the student can begin effectively to explore and discover new principles in a more open fashion. With elementary school children, such open exploration can be guided by appropriately sequenced subject-matter materials.

Curriculum materials that make explicit a growing competence in a subject matter can be quite helpful to the student and the teacher. If the prerequisite knowledges and skills for a level of learning are explicitly indicated, then a child who is unsuccessful at the moment in attaining this level of performance can work on the necessary prerequisites before trying again. Or, a child can move on to a more complex objective under the assumption that learning or the attempt to learn a more complex skill will bring some insight to the prerequisite skill. Or, there can be lateral movement so that what is being learned may be viewed from different perspectives and approached in different ways.

Curriculum materials that permit movement in various directions facilitate the kind of testing and trial that is necessary for the instructional process to be sensitive to individual requirements and to pose motivating challenges. When a child is having difficulty learning a task, the teacher or the child may decompose the task into simpler elements; when a child finds a task too simple, it can be composed into a slightly more complex form. This kind of adjustment is difficult to carry out on the spot in the classroom unless appropriately designed curriculum materials are available. (Principles and examples relating to the organization of sequential learning hierarchies are described in Gagné [1962, 1970] and in Resnick, Wang, and Kaplan [1973], and some illustrations are discussed in Chapters 5 and 6.)

Curriculum materials designed in an explicitly modular, progressive fashion are major components of an environment that fosters adaptive individualized instruction. They permit the kind of flexibility required for matching materials to individual needs, accomplishments, and interests. The progression of concepts and skills needs to be explicit enough to pinpoint particular learning problems and to make certain that adequate learning and mastery of certain concepts have occurred before progressing to more complex concepts and skills. Curriculum materials should assist the teacher in the careful diagnostic-prescriptive guidance that a child might require.

The kinds of materials required for adaptive instruction contrast with the kinds of texts and lesson materials that are generally currently available in elementary school education. These conventional materials assume that the teacher presents new concepts in group instruction and that the children's exercises serve largely as practice for the group. At the present time, most classroom materials encourage the continuation of group-oriented rather than student-centered instruction, and adaptation to individual needs by the teacher's art and by the participation of the student in self-guided work is restricted. In general, for an effectively adaptive environment for learning, the competing merits of different curricula should be judged to a significant degree by the extent to which they are related to and adjustable to differences among learners.

Matching Children and Instruction, and Making Instructional Decisions

Matching the progress of children to the work they perform in school is a pervasive aspect of an adaptive educational approach. Specifically, matching refers to the task of relating student capabilities, acquired knowledge, and skills to particular school activities. Matching decisions are made by the teacher and the student, and are facilitated by curriculum materials and the structure of the classroom. The matching process is also facilitated by the specification of instructional goals in terms of observable student performance and by the utilization of tests and observations for the placement of children in a curriculum sequence according to their level of achievement. The principle involved is the keying of instructional materials to tests and teacher observations so that assignments can be made on the basis of information about children's performance.

Overall, the effectiveness of the process of matching is dependent upon appropriate and timely information being available to all individuals concerned: The student receives information about his or her particular strengths and weaknesses; the teacher observes details of the student's performance and makes direct assignments where necessary, turns over assignment selection to the student where desirable, or works together with the student to make a decision about the next instructional steps; supervisors and school administrators may observe and facilitate information flow and decision making where necessary. Key aspects of the matching process are: (a) that the information focuses on interests and accomplishments actually exhibited by students and not on achievement just assumed to exist as a result of prior school attendance; and (b) that the available instructional options are displayed in a way that permits ready accessibility.

Making decisions about instructional activities—new assignments, next lessons and projects, structured work or free exploration—becomes highlighted in the individualized classroom because these decisions are made on an individual basis and in a more fine-grained way than they are in classrooms with overall class assignments or daily class lesson plans. Good decisions are made on the basis of good information that is frequently updated. On the basis of what is initially known about a child, a tentative decision is made; additional information is gathered as the child is observed in school, and the decision is sustained or adjusted accordingly. Appropriate, frequent adjustments in the instructional process can then be made so that there is constant and dynamic adaptation to performance.

Assessment Procedures

In order to provide the kind of information required for making instructional decisions, tests and assessment procedures need to have certain general characteristics. These measurements need to provide information on how well a student is performing in relation to certain desired goals or objectives. Through this information, both the teacher and the student become aware of the ways in which performance meets, exceeds, or falls short of certain criteria of accomplishment. This information needs to be related to specific content and processes of performance. It should not merely indicate that one student is performing better than another on some normative basis, that one student is, for example, in the 90th percentile and another in the 70th percentile. Instead, tests should be interpreted by students and teachers as a means for providing them with information to guide further instruction, and not as devices to be used only for evaluation and grading.

The information obtained from tests should refer to details of performance that suggest decisions about various instructional options and other learning activities. When interpreted in this way, tests can be regarded much more openly than is currently the case. Sample tests could be examined in advance by students who will eventually take them, and thereby serve to display the competencies that the students are to acquire.

For both the teacher and the student, the classroom must be supplied with appropriate procedures and materials for gathering information about the progress of learning. These include: (a) pretests, which indicate how much a student knows before beginning new lessons and whether he or she needs to brush up on prerequisites or can skip certain lessons and move on to more advanced work; (b) curriculum-embedded tests and opportunities for observation during the course of learning, whereby a child's progress may be observed so that feedback can be given on the adequacy of his or her performance; and (c) posttests, which serve as opportunities for the student to display his or her newly learned competence so that there is some assurance of the attainment and retention of skills and knowledge.

Curriculum Maps

Decision making requires not only information about the performance and progress of a child, but also knowledge of the available instructional options. For this purpose, a "map" of the curriculum that displays the various learning experiences related to different curriculum objectives is very useful. When a child is working on a particular objective at a particular point in the curriculum, both the teacher and the child need to know what prerequisites are required for successful learning of this objective. If the student is not progressing well, the teacher can decide, assisted by diagnostic tests if necessary, what prerequisite skills need to be developed or exercised. If a child appears to be learning rapidly and appears to know a good deal about the objective on which he or she is working, the teacher can, based on knowledge of the curriculum structure, assign the student to advanced exercises or to work with an advanced group of students. Given knowledge of the total span of the curriculum objectives, the teacher can guide children's learning according to their interests and progress.

The Self-Management and Cognitive Capabilities for Learning

Since an adaptive instructional environment does not continue the general practice of organizing children into relatively large and constant groupings in which they work through a curriculum at a prescribed rate, new classroom settings are necessary. In these new settings, the classroom scene is changed from one in which the children are passive learners, limited in physical activity, and overly dependent upon external direction, to settings in which children move about, talk with each other, and frequently make judgments and decisions about learning by themselves or in conjunction with their teachers and peers. Consequently, an adaptive classroom environment must be designed so that the learner is able to function to an increasing extent as a responsible person participating in decisions about the course of his or her own education.

In the elementary school, educational responsibility can be fostered early in the kindergarten and primary grades in simple ways, which then gradually become more complex. The central goal is to nurture and develop capabilities of two general kinds: (a) self-management capabilities that include the ability to engage in self-directed learning and exploration that fosters learning; and (b) capabilities that underlie continued cognitive growth in linguistic abilities, perceptual and conceptual skills, problem solving, and related intellectual skills.

Self-Management Capabilities

"Self-management skills" serve a child in preparing, organizing, and carrying out the activities required in an academic task. To function successfully in an individualized school setting, a child must develop competence in these management skills. Specifically, these skills include the ability to engage in self-directed and purposeful exploration of the environment; the ability to set goals and recognize when they have been met; the ability to make decisions and to recognize the consequences of a decision; and a sense of mastery and confidence based upon the ability to exercise control over one's environment in socially mature ways. Certain social skills and attitudes are developed which aid in giving and requesting help to and from others, and which permit participation in group problem-solving activities—a context in which children develop an awareness of their own abilities and those of others.

The design of preschool and primary grade school settings that encourage even very young children to carry out self-management procedures shows how capable children can be in this regard. For example, before children can actually perform any of the tasks on a list that they are expected to complete, they are faced with the problem of obtaining and setting up their work. The skills involved in doing this can be facilitated and learned when a classroom is arranged to encourage their development. Instructional materials can be stored and coded on open shelves. To the teacher, the code on the materials indicates its difficulty level (and therefore its relationship to a child's level of performance) and the particular objectives being taught.

When children are assigned to certain instructional activities, they can exercise management skills such as the following: identifying the appropriate code on a set of lesson materials; going to the correct shelf and systematically looking for and selecting the right materials; if the materials are not present, requesting help or going on to the next task; if the lesson materials are present, checking to see if they are complete and if additional materials are needed; figuring out what is to be done with the materials and determining whether or not assistance is needed. After completing the task, the children ask the teacher to check their work, return the materials to the shelf, and select the next assignment. These skills, simple as they appear to be, are far from trivial, as can be seen when one considers what might occur in a traditional classroom.

In a traditional classroom, a class of 25 to 30 children are seated and quiet as the teacher passes out the materials, asks a particular child to pass them out, or calls on rows of children to go to the shelves to get their materials and return to their places. This is usually followed by a verbal explanation and demonstration of the task to be accomplished by all children. As a result, few self-management skills are acquired, exercised, or initiated by the individual child. Such self-initiating aspects of learning began with simple tasks for young children and can become progressively complex for older children. Classroom environments can be designed for this purpose so that it is easy for teachers to encourage and reinforce the development of self-management skills as a significant way of learning.

Cognitive Capabilities

Placing increased reliance on children's self-learning capabilities brings into focus the cognitive strategies that children use and acquire as they learn the subject matter of the elementary school. The individualization of instruction must emphasize the ways in which children develop learning-to-learn skills, skills of concentration, and problem solving. While teachers have always been concerned with the teaching of such skills, learner-centered programs elevate their importance because of the increased responsibility placed on children to assist in their own instruction.

The teaching of such cognitive capabilities becomes explicit in at least two ways. First, prerequisite abilities that are necessary for more advanced learning can be taught. For example, beginning reading requires certain prerequisite readiness abilities. If these abilities are not adequately developed, they need to be strengthened prior to entrance into beginning reading programs, and the teaching of these specific cognitive processes can become an important part of the kindergarten and first-grade curriculum (Rosner, 1973a). Second, the kind of performance generally accepted as evidence of intelligence and aptitude can be influenced.

Such instruction in cognitive capabilities is intimately tied to the teaching of subject-matter knowledge and skills. As children acquire knowledge and subject-matter literacy, they also learn to think, to solve problems, to explore, and to be creative with respect to the subject matter they are learning. Children learn to think with words as they learn new words and as they learn about the structure of language, writing, and communication. As they acquire knowledge and skill in arithmetic, algebra, and geometry, they learn techniques of mathematical problem solving that are generalizable to other subject-matter areas and aspects of daily living.

An educational environment that encourages the ability to learn on one's own should aspire to teach the cognitive abilities required for continuous high-order learning. These abilities are the prerequisites for learning new knowledge and skills, for intelligently using newly acquired information, and for self-teaching. Curricula that emphasize such capabilities need to be further developed and this is only beginning to be undertaken. Diagnostic tests of cognitive abilities based on recent research in developmental psychology are being developed (e.g., Anderson, Bogatz, Draper, Jungeblut, Sidwell, Ward, & Yates, 1974), and much research is focusing on the cognitive capabilities for self-learning (see Chapter 6).

Teaching Skills

All good teachers develop skills of relating to, working with, and guiding individual students. These skills become highlighted in the adaptive classroom, where there is deemphasis on total class management, which is characteristic of standard classroom practices. An individualized classroom requires that many individual students interact with the teacher or teacher aide in the course of the school day. In order to accomplish this, teachers need to learn efficient and effective techniques for directing, guiding, and encouraging children on a one-to-one basis. Frequent contacts, although they may be brief, can carry much instructional and motivational impact. These contacts can be more appropriate to each child and therefore more effective than large group interaction. An emphasis on brief contacts does not, however, preclude the possibility that both teacher and child have a more sustained contact involving deeper discussions, and mutually warm and respectful interactions.

Sustained interactions between teacher and child and between child and child are very important. Indeed, the opportunity for this interaction needs to be provided as frequently as possible, and its unique merit is not being challenged here. We wish, however, to especially emphasize practices that involve numerous, shorter instructional interactions with students as they proceed in their classroom activities.

On the basis of research and observation of the performance of teachers in a variety of adaptive classrooms, a number of areas of teacher skills have been identified (Leinhardt, 1975). In certain respects, not all these skills are unique to adaptive instruction; good teachers generally have them, but we shall discuss them in terms of their particular salience for the individualized classroom.

Pedagogical Skills

Pedagogical skills presuppose knowledge about the subject matter, the curriculum, and the learner. With respect to the curriculum, the teacher must be knowledgeable about the organization and sequencing of instructional activities, techniques, and options. Information about the curriculum's hierarchy of objectives and skill development enables teachers to answer the following kinds of questions: What skills need to be mastered before other skills? What skills can be learned at the same time? What skills are not necessarily related to one another so that as they are learned, the sequence between them is not crucial? If certain objectives are to be taught and a child has not mastered some of the subskills related to that objective, at what place should instruction begin? Knowledge is also required of the different instructional resources that the curriculum offers—such as workbooks, tapes, manipulative materials, film strips—and which are pertinent to various aspects of what is being learned.

Pedagogical skills also involve knowledge about the learner and the use of that knowledge in teaching. The teacher must be informed about the following: (a) Required prerequisites—

What kind of competence does a child need to have before a new level of competence can be taught? (b) The child's background —What are the child's particular interests, and what is his personal history of learning? (c) The details of the task being carried out—How can a particular exercise or lesson be broken into component tasks so that learning is facilitated for a particular child? (d) The changing state of the student—What are a child's achievement and performance capabilities at a particular point in time?

Monitoring Skills

Obtaining and using information about the learner and the curriculum requires that the teacher monitor and tutor children individually and manage the activities of the classroom. Aspects of monitoring skills include the following: (a) Assessing instructional effects—collecting information on alternate instructional procedures and collecting evidence through observing student performance to ascertain whether these procedures are appropriate. (b) Assessing transfer—determining that a child has not learned "by rote," but is able to generalize specific skills learned in one setting, or from one set of examples, to an unfamiliar setting or to new kinds of problems. (c) Predicting outcomes— judging, on the basis of a student's present performance, how the child will perform on subsequent, more difficult lessons and, on the basis of this prediction, deciding what next instructional steps are appropriate. (d) Observing performance details— focusing on particular features of a child's performance in a particular situation. Is the child attending to the relevant aspects of the problem, or is he or she off on the wrong track?

Tutorial Skills

Tutorial skills involve one-to-one, short-term instructional contacts with every child. These include such aspects as: (a) Prefamiliarization—giving a child prior exposure to the concepts that he or she will learn, and to the objectives of a lesson. With prefamiliarization, the lesson will not be prohibitively novel, and the child can be motivated by anticipating what he or she is to learn. (b) Modeling—demonstrating and working through certain elements of the task to provide the child with examples of what he or she is to do on similar and related problems. (c) Questioning—asking the child questions in a systematic way in order to guide his or her learning. (d) Cueing and prompting —providing verbal and visual information (hints, so to speak) that assist children in solving a problem, and then gradually eliminating such prompts as the child becomes increasingly proficient. (e) Diagnosis—assessing on the spot what the child already knows so that he or she can be moved ahead, or determining what particular momentary inabilities are interfering with learning progress and then, on the basis of this information, making appropriate instructional decisions. (f) Posttesting —confirming the accomplishment of a competence or a learning objective. This involves obtaining appropriate evidence that the child has acquired a particular knowledge item or skill.

Management Skills

Management skills involve the activities of the teacher that are required to keep an individualized classroom running smoothly. They include, but are not limited to, such things as keeping track of the various activities of the children and, on the basis of this information, deciding to group certain students so they can work together or be taught as a group. Management skills also involve keeping records of agreements that have been made with children about their activities, including the particular lessons they plan to complete. In general, management skills contribute to the active involvement of children in the learning process by organizing and reorganizing classroom activities so that children can work by themselves, with one or two others, or in larger groups as is appropriate to a particular subject matter at a particular time.

"Traveling" Skills

Of particular interest in connection with the teaching skills required for individualized instruction is the technique called "traveling," which makes it possible for the teacher to manage individual instructional interactions within a classroom setting. In particular forms of individualized classrooms, examples of which will be presented in Chapter 5, it is generally the case that different children or groups of children are working at many different things at the same time. With such diversity of activity, it becomes a formidable management task for the teacher to work with individual children. In fact, a usual sign of malaise in a teacher trying out an individualized classroom for the first time is the attempt to draw the children back into the standard group instruction format with which the teacher is already proficient. However, once the techniques of individual monitoring and tutoring are mastered, teachers find this style especially rewarding; as they become expert at it, they are disinclined to return to their older instructional mode.

Traveling involves the teacher moving among the students as they are working, and students moving to or signaling the teacher that advice or attention is requested. In carrying out the traveling role, a scheme is devised whereby, in the course of a particular subject-matter period or in the course of a day, the teacher makes contact with all children requiring attention. For example, if they are working, the teacher may stop by to look at their work and praise them. If a child needs his work checked, the teacher stops by to do this or assigns it to a classroom aide. If certain children need help on particular lessons or are not sure of what they are supposed to do, the teacher stops by at their request to assist them with their work. If some children have finished a lesson and would like guidance in moving on to another activity, they can indicate this to the teacher. If certain children are not attending to their work at the moment, the teacher can decide whether to ignore them for the moment or stop to ask them about their current daydream or dilemma.

Teacher attention is important to children, and when they are aware of the activities for which the teacher provides attention and conversation, they will shift their activities to obtain it. The extent of monitoring required and the need for feedback are significant individual differences among children. For example, some children need more questions answered than do others; some need more careful explanation of directions; some need infrequent praise for their accomplishments, while others need very frequent attention and feedback for small accomplishments; and some children initially need much contact and support, which can then be systematically withdrawn as they become more self-sustained. The information that students receive about their performance, from their own observation or through a teacher, regulates future learning activities. The teacher needs to observe the activity of children so that feedback consequent to this activity can be given.

These important instructional contacts with students take but a few moments of time, and the teacher learns to use these few moments with great effectiveness and insight that is rewarding both to the teacher and to the child. In comparison to less dynamic forms of teaching, these frequent, short-term contacts add up to a great deal of individual guidance.

Summary

In this chapter, we have attempted to describe principles and practices that can assist educators in moving toward more flexible school programs. To accomplish this, an elementary school should be designed so that time boundaries and grade levels are treated as flexible entities; educational materials and curricula are highly modular with flexible points of entry and branches for advancement, exploration, and review. Performance is carefully monitored so that adaptation can be made to a child's progress, and individual diagnosis and evaluation is emphasized, in contrast to general class assessment. Levels of learning are defined in terms of the degree of competence to be achieved, and tests and assessment procedures primarily provide information adequate for individual instructional guidance. Children control their paths of learning either because the teacher adjusts to their abilities and interests or because they can do so through their own self-management. Abilities such as self-management and cognitive processes like problem solving and inquiry become explicit subject matters of elementary school education. Acting on these general principles involves the creative efforts of teachers, school administrators, curriculum designers, test developers, and the trainers of teachers.

The next chapter presents an array of examples of various curricula and classroom practices that have been developed with the principles of adaptive education in mind. As experience is obtained and as the results of various practices become evident, they can be adjusted in accordance with their success in attaining the ends and objectives of elementary schooling. While the means employed should be the best that we can offer our children, they still represent practices that are to be continually improved. Educational practices are best viewed as open to constant adjustment on the basis of informed observation of their effects.

Chapter 5 Examples from the Primary School

I wish that practising was not
so different from preaching.

John Godfrey Saxe, circa 1850

This chapter illustrates how the general principles and practices
described in Chapter 4 might be realized in actual practice. Preschool and elementary school programs are presented as examples. The curricula described were developed by individuals
at the Learning Research and Development Center, University
of Pittsburgh, as part of a long-range effort to design and study
adaptive education in the elementary school. The programs were
developed in conjunction with several elementary school systems and involved the cooperative efforts of teachers, students,
school administrators, and university research and development
specialists. These curricula are approximations toward evolving
educational ideals, and as such work proceeds, the principles
and practices involved should become more articulated. Furthermore, as actual school realizations are studied and tested, and
more knowledge is obtained, the specific characteristics of these
programs can be modified and changed.

Described in this chapter are a classroom organization and
management system, a preschool program, a beginning reading
program, and an elementary school science curriculum. Each of
these programs can function as a separate entity, or all may be
coordinated for use in an elementary school classroom. It is in
the latter context that they are presented here.

Managing Learning and Instruction

The Self-Schedule System (Resnick, Wang, & Rosner, in press; Wang, 1974) is a classroom organization and management system designed for learner-centered programs and for developing children's ability to plan and manage their own learning. This system is especially designed for use with curricula that combine structured, teacher-prescribed learning tasks with open-ended, child-selected activities.

Students in classrooms operating under the Self-Schedule System obtain their assignments at the beginning of a session and decide with the teacher the amount of time they need to complete prescribed tasks. They may, however, work on the tasks in any order they plan, and may choose to mix work on prescribed tasks with self-selected exploratory activities. During the course of the day, the teacher may assemble certain children for group activities or group instruction, or may tutor, counsel, or test children individually on their work. Following these activities, the children return to their planned activities, continuing to work in their own style and at their own pace.

Learning To Plan

This system requires that students share the control of and responsibility for their own learning. Figure 5.1 shows a hierarchy of levels in the development of a student's ability to plan his or her learning activities under the Self-Schedule System. Each level is stated in terms of the student's competence in a given situation. As a student progresses from the initial level (A and B) to more complex levels, the conditions of choice become more complex in that the number of tasks to be completed increases, the time to be planned lengthens (from one hour to one week), and the range of task options broadens (prescriptive, exploratory, or both; one, several, or many subject areas). Mastery of each level further extends a child's abilities to estimate the time needed to complete various tasks and activities; allocate a period of time, considering task requirements and his or her abilities and interests; postpone or forego self-selected activities to ensure completion of prescribed tasks; modify or revise his or her plans in light of unexpected inter-

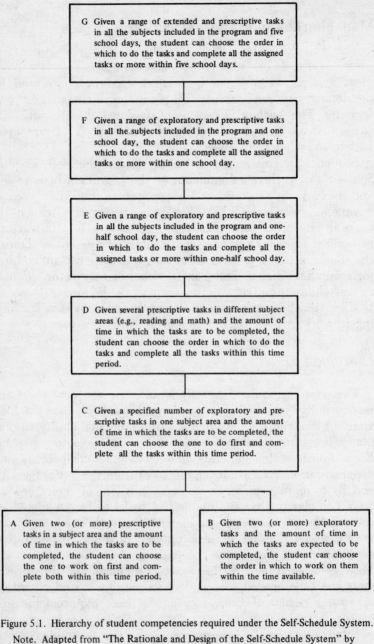

G Given a range of extended and prescriptive tasks in all the subjects included in the program and five school days, the student can choose the order in which to do the tasks and complete all the assigned tasks or more within five school days.

F Given a range of exploratory and prescriptive tasks in all the subjects included in the program and one school day, the student can choose the order in which to do the tasks and complete all the assigned tasks or more within one school day.

E Given a range of exploratory and prescriptive tasks in all the subjects included in the program and one-half school day, the student can choose the order in which to do the tasks and complete all the assigned tasks or more within one-half school day.

D Given several prescriptive tasks in different subject areas (e.g., reading and math) and the amount of time in which the tasks are to be completed, the student can choose the order in which to do the tasks and complete all the tasks within this time period.

C Given a specified number of exploratory and prescriptive tasks in one subject area and the amount of time in which the tasks are to be completed, the student can choose the one to do first and complete all the tasks within this time period.

A Given two (or more) prescriptive tasks in a subject area and the amount of time in which the tasks are to be completed, the student can choose the one to work on first and complete both within this time period.

B Given two (or more) exploratory tasks and the amount of time in which the tasks are expected to be completed, the student can choose the order in which to work on them within the time available.

Figure 5.1. Hierarchy of student competencies required under the Self-Schedule System.

Note. Adapted from "The Rationale and Design of the Self-Schedule System" by M. C. Wang (Pittsburgh: University of Pittsburgh, Learning Research and Development Center, 1974).

ruptions or difficulties; and experiment with various kinds of plans (e.g., complete all prescriptive or all exploratory tasks, or mix exploratory with prescriptive tasks).

Following such a hierarchy as a guide, a teacher introduces a child to the procedure of self-scheduling by having the child work at initial levels (A or B). Working at Level A means that the teacher prescribes two tasks, specifies that the tasks should be completed in an hour, and explains to the child that he or she can choose the order in which to work and complete the tasks. At Level B, the teacher gives the child the opportunity to choose two exploratory activities (games, sociodramatic play, painting, etc.), specifies that they be completed in an hour, and explains that the child should plan his or her work.

After competence at Level B is shown, the child is presented with a situation representative of Level C: The teacher prescribes two tasks in one subject area (e.g., reading), provides the opportunity to choose two exploratory activities related to that subject area, specifies that all four tasks and activities are to be completed in two hours, and explains that the child can choose to work on and complete them in any order. When the child masters a level, he or she moves up in the hierarchy to the next level. At any point, the time or activities assigned can be adjusted to individual requirements. The time required for an individual child to attain the higher levels of self-management competence depends upon the rate at which he or she achieves the competencies at each sublevel. Generally, however, in three to five weeks in the classroom, four-year-olds can be expected to achieve Level E; five- and six-year-olds, Level F; and seven-year-olds, Level G (Wang, 1974).

With the Self-Schedule System, then, learning activities and tasks are not assigned by the teacher to be undertaken by the whole class at specified times. Instead, each child plans activities for a day or week in consultation with the teacher. Each child's plan includes the tasks prescribed by the teacher and a selection of exploratory activities chosen by the child with guidance from the teacher. Self-scheduling provides opportunities for flexibility in matching instruction to an individual's needs and interests, enables and requires a child to assume increased responsibility for his or her learning, and requires teachers to instruct and guide individuals engaged in a variety of activities. The functions of teachers in this kind of flexible learning environment and the procedures for carrying out these functions have been described generally in Chapter 4, and more specific illustrations are provided later in this chapter. So, too, are examples of how curricula in various subject-matter areas manage and make use of the flexibility provided by such environments. In the remainder of this section on managing learning and instruction, we discuss how the arrangement of the classroom can facilitate children taking responsibility for their own learning.

Support for Self-Scheduling

For children to make choices among alternative learning activities and to devise plans of study, it is necessary that they know what options and resources are available. Furthermore, a classroom full of children simultaneously working at various levels of a variety of subject-matter curricula or engaging in a diverse range of exploratory activities requires that children be able to identify, obtain, and use materials with minimal assistance from the teacher. In general, these requirements can be met by utilizing classroom space to create specific, well-defined activity areas. There might be areas, for example, for work on various prescriptive components in reading, math, and science; areas for engaging in exploratory activities involving experimentation and investigation in these subject matters; and areas that provide opportunities for integrating and applying learned competencies to more practical situations that cut across subject-matter boundaries, such as creative art, sociodramatic play, and conceptual games.

Physical space. Traditional elementary school classrooms are often arranged with rows of individual student desks and few clearly defined areas for special activities. This arrangement is well suited to an instructional mode in which a teacher instructs a class as a whole, students have little responsibility for their own learning, and students spend most of their time working at their desks. A room can be rearranged, however, and the space can be effectively used to facilitate a more flexible mode of instruction and learning, as shown in Figure 5.2.

In a more adaptive environment, certain features can be noted:

(a) The rows of individual student desks are gone. Some desks are retained, but they are pushed together to form large work surfaces that encourage group activities and interaction among students working in an activity area. In addition, there are tables throughout the room for individual work.

(b) Each activity area is clearly defined. Bookshelves form the areas and partially partition each area from other areas. The shelves are used to store or display materials, and pegboards can be attached to the backs of them.

(c) Within each area, there is room for storing, displaying, and using materials. The materials in each area include those needed for both prescribed and related exploratory activities.

(d) Areas are arranged to encourage integration of activities and permit ready sharing of equipment and materials. Thus, for example, the math and science areas are adjacent, and science and social studies are in the same area.

(e) The open floor space permits and encourages children to move freely about the room and provides a large work space. Children may bring materials from the defined areas and work on the floor or on rugs.

Figure 5.2 provides general suggestions for arranging a classroom to support an adaptive environment. As with the use of time, the use of space can be adapted to students' needs and interests, the demands of curricula used in the classroom, and the style of the teacher. The use of movable furniture provides the flexibility required for relatively easy experimentation and modification.

Access to materials. There are two aspects to providing children with access to instructional materials. One involves the storage and display of materials in the activity areas, and the other involves children's access to the activity areas. In general, each area contains the materials and equipment needed to engage in the activities of that area. For the prescriptive components of a program, the materials may be stored in boxes keyed to instructional assignments so that children can match the code on their assignment sheet with the box needed for a particular task or activity. (See Chapter 4 for additional dis-

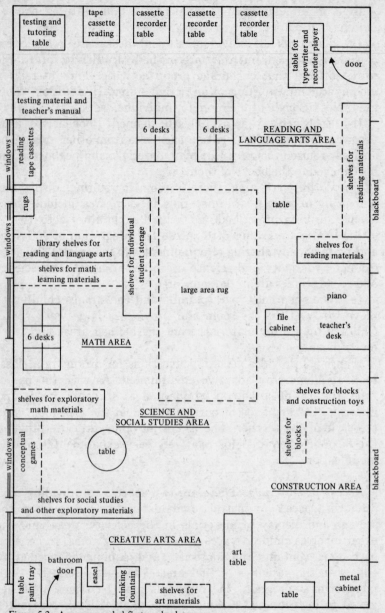

Figure 5.2. A recommended first-grade classroom.

Note. Adapted from "Teacher's Manual for the Exploratory Learning Component of the LRDC Individualized Instructional Program for the Early Learning Grades" (Vol. 1) by M. C. Wang (Pittsburgh: University of Pittsburgh, Learning Research and Development Center, 1973).

cussion of the notion of materials display.) Materials for exploratory activities are also stored in appropriate activity areas and are displayed on open shelves. With this open display arrangement, children are encouraged to observe and handle the materials and experiment and make discoveries. Children can learn how to use the materials either through explicit demonstration by the teacher or through observing more experienced children.

Access to activity areas is controlled in two ways. The teacher has some control through the assignments of tasks and activities given to children. Since, however, children plan their own days or weeks under the Self-Schedule System, there must be additional means for ensuring that activity areas are not overcrowded. One way to do this is to have a pegboard showing each area by name (and perhaps, by color code). Under the name of each area there is a number of hooks corresponding to the number of children that the area can accommodate. When children go to work in an area, they place their name tags on a hook under the appropriate area name. In this way, both the teacher and the children can see at a glance which areas are free and where each child is working. When a child encounters a situation in which an area is filled, he or she must decide whether to wait for a vacancy or to modify his or her plan and go on to something else for the time being.

A system of this kind provides an environmentally designed management tool whereby the various components of an elementary school program can be very flexibly implemented. We now turn to describing some possible curriculum components of such a system.

An Early Learning Program

The Primary Education Project (PEP) (Resnick, Wang, & Rosner, in press) was designed for children from preschool through the early primary grades. The preschool, which was the initial focus of the project's work, is discussed here. PEP is based on the concept that cognitive development proceeds in an essentially hierarchical fashion; certain abilities appear earlier than others, and early appearing abilities comprise building blocks or prerequisites for acquiring more complex abilities. Mature concepts and skills are acquired in successive stages—

stages that must be clarified if instruction is optimally matched
to the learner.

Most psychologists agree that cognitive development proceeds in a hierarchical, ordered way, but they disagree on the
kinds of cognitive skills to be taught, the methods of teaching
to be used, and, in general, how cognitive development is influenced. The sequential development of cognitive abilities under-
lies Piaget's notion of cognitive stages and of Gagné's behavior-
ally oriented theory of cumulative learning (see Chapter 6 for a
discussion of the latter). Both approaches share belief in the
mutually interacting influence of organismic and environmental
events in the development of cognitive competence. Most
Piagetians, however, are "noninterventionist" and emphasize the
acquisition of general abilities. They stress the natural sequence
of development and the role of "general experience" (Kohlberg,
1968) in providing the child with events that eventually lead to
the development of new cognitive abilities. It is difficult, therefore, to draw specific guidelines for instructional design based on
Piagetian and related theories.

Cumulative learning theory attempts to break "general experience" apart and identify the events that are most critical
in producing cognitive growth. The assumption is that once
these events can be identified, a child's cognitive development
can be influenced by providing specific instructional experiences
that are matched to a child's existing states of competence. PEP
bridges these two approaches. The program assumes that
matches can be made, and espouses a form of cumulative learning theory as a guideline for generating curricula. In addition,
PEP accepts the goal of developing generalized rather than
specific abilities, and thereby shares with Piagetian theorists a
concern for the acquisition of general concepts and cognitive
abilities.

Curriculum Objectives

Three classes of abilities are included in the PEP curriculum
(Resnick, 1967)—perceptual-motor skills, conceptual and linguistic skills, and orienting and attending skills. Perceptual-
motor skills are the processing competencies a child needs to
analyze and synthesize visual and auditory information—the

skills necessary in beginning stages of school learning. Included are complex auditory and visual analysis skills for extracting information effectively from instructional materials and from the general environment. Also included is a variety of gross- and fine-motor skills. Conceptual-linguistic skills include classification, reasoning, and memory skills, and general cognitive abilities that children acquire and use as they learn the basic subject matter of elementary school.

Orienting and attending skills involve a variety of personal work habits, including the abilities to concentrate on a task and resist distractions, to attend to appropriate details and to follow directions, and to accept delayed rather than immediate concrete rewards. These skills also include motivational traits such as confidence in one's ability to succeed, willingness to attempt new tasks, and feelings of pride in completing tasks rather than leaving them unfinished. Related to these latter abilities are certain social skills such as accepting and giving help. The PEP program considers these orienting and attending skills prerequisite to all other skills in an early learning program. It is sensitive to the fact that some children need time to experience accomplishment in these areas before other curricula can be very effectively introduced in a progam like this one, which attempts to develop effective learning-to-learn skills in the course of subject-matter learning.

Content

The objectives of the PEP program are met by using a combination of structured curricula and informal, child-selected activities. The structured curricula include programs in perceptual-motor skills, classification, and quantification. Informal, exploratory, problem-solving activities are geared to these three curriculum areas. Generalized skills, like communication and social interaction, and orienting and attending skills, are developed through the use of the system of classroom organization and teacher-child relationships described in the previous section on the Self-Schedule System.

The curriculum content of the program is organized into an explicit set of target abilities and a series of steps that can successively develop these abilities. Hierarchies of specific capabilities serve as the basis for ordering learning experiences and matching a child's developing competence enroute to achieving the target abilities—achievements that constitute an acceptable level of cognitive competence for a six- or seven-year-old. These curriculum sequences display for the teacher (and child) prerequisite performances; the presence or absence of these prerequisites can facilitate or hinder a child's acquisition of the objectives of the program (Resnick, 1973; Resnick, Wang, & Kaplan, 1973). A discussion of hierarchy analysis for the purposes of curriculum development is described more fully in Chapter 6.

The quantification and classification curricula. The Quantification Curriculum is an introductory mathematics curriculum that presents fundamental operations that serve as a foundation for later work. The curriculum is organized around the core concept of "number"; the curriculum objectives are listed in Table 5.1. It should not be inferred from the listing of these objectives that all children follow a fixed, linear path of learning. Rather, the objectives are organized in hierarchies that permit multiple learning paths that are constrained by prerequisite relations among the objectives.

The hierarchical relationships among the units of Table 5.1 are shown in Figure 5.3, and the pattern of relationships among the objectives of each unit is shown in Figure 5.4. The units to be learned first appear at the bottom of these charts and are prerequisite to those appearing above and connected by a line. In Figure 5.3, for example, Unit 1 is prerequisite to 2 and 3; Units 2 and 3, however, are not prerequisite to each other and need not be taught one before the other, but can be taught in either order. Unit 5 has two prerequisites, 2 and 4, and is not normally taught until both these units are mastered.

The Classification Curriculum is organized in similar fashion. The objectives of the curriculum include abilities in matching, sorting, and labeling. The objectives and units are listed in Table 5.2, and the hierarchical relationship between the units is shown in Figure 5.5.

The perceptual skills curriculum. The Perceptual Skills Curriculum (Rosner, 1972, 1973b) is comprised of three compo-

Table 5.1 Objectives of the PEP Quantification Curriculum

	GIVEN:	THE CHILD CAN:
Units 1 and 2 Counting and One-to-One Correspondence[a]	A. Sets of up to 5 objects or up to 10 objects B. Set of moveable objects C. Fixed ordered set of objects D. Fixed unordered set of objects E. A numeral stated and a set of objects F. A numeral stated and several sets of fixed objects G. Two sets of objects H. Two unequal sets of objects I. Two unequal sets of objects	A. Recite the numerals in order B. Count the objects, moving them out of the set as he counts C. Count ordered set of objects D. Count the objects E. Count out a subset of stated size F. Select a set of size indicated by numeral G. Pair objects and state whether the sets are equivalent H. Pair objects and state which set has more I. Pair objects and state which set has less
Units 3 and 4 Numerals[b]	A. Two sets of numerals B. A numeral stated, and a set of printed numerals C. A numeral (written) D. Several sets of objects and several numerals E. Two numerals (written) F. A set of numerals G. Numerals stated	A. Match the numerals B. Select the stated numeral C. Read the numeral D. Match numerals with appropriate sets E. State which shows more (less) F. Place them in order G. Write the numeral
Unit 5 Comparison of Sets	A. Two sets of objects B. Two sets of objects C. A set of objects and a numeral D. A numeral and several sets of objects A set of objects and several numerals E. Two rows of objects (not paired) F. Three sets of objects	A. Count sets and state which has more objects or that sets have same number B. Count sets and state which has less objects C. State which shows more (less) D. Select sets which are more (less) than the numeral Select numerals which show more (less) than the set of objects E. State which row has more regardless of arrangement F. Count sets and state which has most (least)
Unit 6 Seriation and Ordinal Position	A. Three objects of different sizes B. Objects of graduated sizes C. Several sets of objects D. Ordered set of objects	A. Select the largest (smallest) B. Seriate according to size C. Seriate the sets according to size of objects D. Name the ordinal position of the objects
Unit 7 Addition and Subtraction (sums to 10)	A. Two numbers stated, set of objects, and directions to add B. Two numbers stated, set of objects, and directions to subtract C. Two numbers stated, number line, and directions to add D. Two numbers stated, number line, and directions to subtract E. Addition and subtraction word problems F. Written addition and subtraction problems in form: $\frac{x}{+y}$ or $\frac{y}{-y}$ G. Addition and subtraction problems in the form: $x + y =$ or $x - y =$	A. Add the numbers by counting out two subsets then combining and stating combined number as sum B. Count out smaller subset from larger and state remainder C. Use the number line to determine sum D. Use number line to subtract E. Solve the problems F. Complete the problems G. Complete the equations

[a]Unit 1 involves sets of up to 5 objects; Unit 2 involves sets of up to 10 objects.
[b]Unit 3 involves numerals and sets of up to 5 objects; Unit 4 involves numerals and sets of up to 10 objects.

Note. Adapted from "Adaptive Education for Young Children: The Primary Education Project" by L. B. Resnick, M. C. Wang, and J. Rosner. In The Preschool in Action: Exploring Early Childhood Programs (2nd ed.) edited by M. C. Day and R. K. Parker (Boston: Allyn & Bacon, 1976).

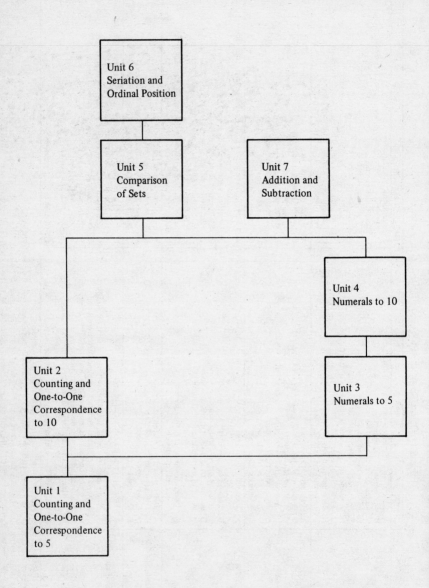

Figure 5.3. Hierarchical relations between the units of the PEP Quantification Program.

Note. Adapted from "Adaptive Education for Young Children: The Primary Education Project" by L. B. Resnick, M. C. Wang, and J. Rosner. In The Preschool in Action: Exploring Early Childhood Programs (2nd ed.) edited by M. C. Day and R. K. Parker (Boston: Allyn & Bacon, 1976).

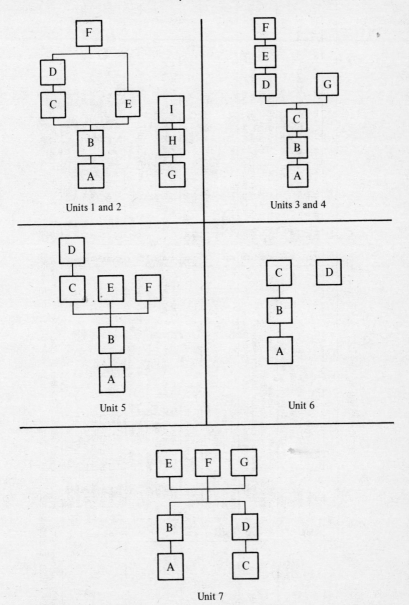

Figure 5.4. Hierarchical relations among the objectives of each unit of the PEP Quantification program.

Note. Adapted from "Adaptive Education for Young Children: The Primary Education Project" by L. B. Resnick, M. C. Wang, and J. Rosner. In <u>The Preschool in Action: Exploring Early Childhood Programs</u> (2nd ed.) edited by M. C. Day and R. K. Parker (Boston: Allyn & Bacon, 1976).

Table 5.2

Objectives of the PEP Classification Curriculum

	GIVEN:	THE CHILD CAN:
Unit 1 Basic Matching Skills	A. A set of two objects B. Two identical sets of objects C. An array of objects varying in one dimension D. Three objects -- two identical, one different E. A sample object and three disimilar objects	A. State whether the pairs are the "same" or "different" B. Pair identical objects C. Sort on the basis of differing attributes of that dimension D. Identify the one that is different E. Identify the one that matches the sample
Unit 2 Shape and Size Discrimination	A. Basic shapes and matching outlines B. Irregular shapes and matching outlines C. Two sizes of rods and instructions to superimpose D. Two sizes of a shape and instructions to superimpose	A. Place the shapes on the appropriate outlines B. Place the shapes on the appropriate outlines C. State whether same or different size and give reason D. State whether same or different size and give reason
Unit 3 Color Naming	A. An array of the basic colors B. An array of the basic colors C. Two identical sets of objects of different shades of a color D. Several shades of a single color	A. Identify the stated colors B. Name the colors C. Match identical objects D. Seriate in order from darkest to lightest
Unit 4 Shape Naming	A. An array of the seven basic shapes B. An array of the seven basic shapes	A. Identify named shape B. Name the shapes
Unit 5 Advanced Matching Skills	A. Two objects, same on one dimension, but different on another B. Three objects, varying in three dimensions, two alike on a given dimension and one different on that given dimension C. A sample object and a set of objects varying in two dimensions D. An array of objects varying in two dimensions, and instructions to sort on the basis of one dimension (e.g., color, shape, size)	A. State whether the objects are the same or different and give reason B. Identify the object that is different and give reason C. Identify object that matches sample in one dimension and give reasons D. Place objects in groups according to one dimension and explain the basis for the sort
Units 6 - 9 Big and Little Long and Short Tall and Short Wide and Narrow	A. Two objects different in size B. Two objects different in size C. Two objects different in size D. Two objects different in size E. Two objects different in size F. Two objects different in size G. Several sizes of an object	A. Point to the "big," ("long," "tall," "wide") object B. Verbally state which object is "big," etc., when asked C. Identify the "little" ("short," "narrow") object D. State which object is "little," etc., when asked E. Describe according to size, using the term "big," or "little," etc. F. Compare and state which is "bigger," "smaller," etc. G. Seriate in order from biggest to smallest

Note. Adapted from "Adaptive Education for Young Children: The Primary Education Project" by L. B. Resnick, M. C. Wang, and J. Rosner.
In The Preschool in Action: Exploring Early Childhood Programs (2nd ed.) edited by M. C. Day and R. K. Parker (Boston: Allyn & Bacon, 1976).

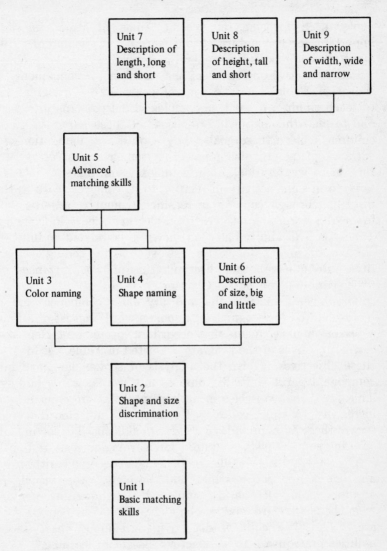

Figure 5.5. Hierarchical relations between the units of the PEP Classification program.

Note. Adapted from "Adaptive Education for Young Children: The Primary Education Project" by L. B. Resnick, M. C. Wang and J. Rosner. In The Preschool in Action: Exploring Early Childhood Programs (2nd ed.) edited by M. C. Day and R. K. Parker (Boston: Allyn & Bacon, 1976).

nents, each focusing on specific kinds of readiness skills important for elementary school learning—visual-motor skills, auditory-motor skills, and general-motor skills.

Representative objectives of the visual-motor component are shown in Table 5.3. The general goals of this program are to teach children to analyze complex visual patterns into parts and to map the spatial interrelations of those parts. As young children achieve these goals, they acquire the foundations for extracting and organizing patterns from a spatial array; i.e., they learn what to look at in complex visual material in order to perform some activity in relation to it. Children learn in this program through copying increasingly complex patterns with fewer and fewer spatial cues to guide them, as is indicated in Table 5.3. This ability has been shown to be related, in different degrees, to early mathematics tasks such as the coding of quantities into numerals and discrimination of the differences between various symbols (see Chapter 3).

The general goals of the auditory skills component are to teach children to recognize that spoken words consist of a finite series of phonic elements that occur in a specific way. Representative objectives of the program are listed in Table 5.4. Most of these objectives involve the analysis of spoken language into component parts—initially, phrases into words; words into syllables; and then syllables into phonemes that are embedded in increasingly complex contexts. Research has indicated that mastery of these tasks provides a child with skills used in sorting and ordering sounds—skills required for learning to read and spell.

The general-motor skills component is concerned with gross- and fine-motor processes that underlie higher-order visual and auditory skills such as are employed in handwriting, copying from the chalkboard, and speech articulation. The general goals are to assist the child as needed in developing sensory-motor abilities prerequisite to satisfactory classroom learning.

Exploratory activities. The structured curricula just described are complemented by learning experiences in which children are encouraged to integrate and further develop their cognitive skills by engaging in self-selected and self-defined activities, and by interacting with peers in the course of learning tasks (see Wang, 1973a, 1973b). These exploratory activities include

Table 5.3

Representative Objectives of the Visual-Motor Component of the Perceptual Skills Curriculum

Level B:

Unit 1: Given a group of one-inch cubes arranged into an interlocking row and column, superimpose matching cubes.

Unit 2: Given a group of one-inch cubes arranged into an interlocking row and column, construct a replication alongside model.

Unit 3: Given a drawing of a group of one-inch cubes arranged into interlocking rows and columns, construct a matching arrangement alongside drawing.

Level D

Unit 1: Given a drawing of a Design Board D on which two rubber bands (one vertical, one horizontal) have been stretched, superimpose two additional rubber bands.

Unit 2: Given a Design Board D on which two rubber bands (one vertical, one horizontal) have been stretched, replicate pattern on second Design Board D.

Unit 3: Given a drawing of a Design Board D* on which two rubber bands (one horizontal, one vertical) are represented, construct the pattern on a second Design Board D**.

Unit 4: Given a drawing of a Design Board D on which three rubber bands (one horizontal, two vertical) are represented, copy (draw) the pattern on a second printed representation of the Design Board D.

Level F

Unit 3: Given a drawing of Design Board F on which three rubber bands (one vertical, two diagonal) are represented, construct the pattern on a Design Board F.

Unit 4: Given a drawing of Design Board F*(on which three rubber bands (one horizontal, one vertical, one diagonal) are represented, copy (draw) the pattern on a second printed representation of Design Board F**.

Level I

Unit 4: Given a drawing of Design Board I on which ten rubber bands (horizontal, vertical, diagonal) are represented, copy (draw) the pattern on a second printed representation of Design Board I.

Unit 5: Given a drawing of Design Board I on which ten rubber bands (vertical, horizontal, diagonal) are represented, copy (draw) the pattern on a second printed representation of Design Board I from which all dots have been faded.

D*

D**

F*

F**

Note. Adapted from "The Development and Validation of an Individualized Perceptual Skills Curriculum" by J. Rosner (Pittsburgh: University of Pittsburgh, Learning Research and Development Center, 1972).

Table 5.4

Representative Objectives of the Visual-Motor Component of the Perceptual Skills Curriculum

Level B

Unit 1: Given music with changing tempo, clap hands in synchrony with the music, adapting to changes in tempo.

Unit 2: Given a series of long and short musical tones, ranging from one to four in total, draw an appropriate horizontal dash for each sound, from left to right.

Unit 3: Given a series of long and short claps, ranging from one to four in total, reproduce the clapping pattern.

Unit 4: Given a spoken phrase of numerals, clap hands once for each word in the phrase.

Unit 5: Given a spoken phrase of numerals, "write" the phrase, using a horizontal dash to represent each numeral (from left to right), and "read" aloud any numeral on request.

Level D

Unit 4: Given a spoken phrase of one- and two-syllable words, say and clap hands simultaneously for each syllable in phrase.

Unit 5: Given a spoken phrase of one- and two-syllable words, "write" the phrase, using a horizontal dash (from left to right) to represent each syllable, and "read" aloud any syllable on request.

Unit 6: Given a spoken two-syllable word, indicate presence or absence of a specified syllable in that word.

Unit 7: Given a spoken two-syllable word followed by a statement of only one of the syllables, say the syllable that was omitted.

Unit 8: Given a spoken two-word series or compound two-syllable word, state single remaining word or syllable by omitting the other as designated.

Level F

Unit 6: Given three spoken words and a specified consonant or vowel sound, indicate which word begins with that sound.

Unit 7: Given a spoken word, followed by a restatement of the word with the initial consonant sound omitted, state the omitted sound.

Unit 8: Given a spoken word, repeat the word omitting its initial consonant sound.

Level H

Unit 6: Given three spoken words and a specified consonant or vowel sound, identify which word contains that sound.

Unit 7: Given a spoken word, followed by a restatement of the word with one consonant sound of a two-consonant blend omitted, state the omitted sound.

Unit 8: Given a spoken word, repeat the word omitting one consonant sound of a two-consonant blend.

Unit 9: Given a spoken word, substitute any consonant or vowel sound for another.

Note: Adapted from "The Development and Validation of an Individualized Perceptual Skills Curriculum" by J. Rosner (Pittsburgh: University of Pittsburgh, Learning Research and Development Center, 1972).

special projects, which encourage extended activity around a particular theme or problem, and conceptual games designed to give practice that integrates concepts taught separately in the prescriptive curricula.

There are also differentiated activity centers in the classroom where materials for the particular activities are available for self-selected use by children. The activities frequently involve two or more children, and the centers are designed to accommodate groups of varying numbers. In these exploratory activities, the teacher interacts with the student in a less direct manner than in the prescriptive curricula, intervening only to give directions where necessary, to pose questions, or to set problems that relate different activities to one another.

Organization of Learning Activities

The classroom environment and instructional procedures in PEP are designed to accomplish two main goals in the context of the curriculum content described above. First, a system of diagnosis and assessment is provided to help teachers adapt the program to individual needs. At one level, this adaptation means assuring that children are not required to repeat tasks they have already mastered nor to work on objectives for which they lack critical prerequisites. At a more general level, this means adapting to individual learning styles and interests, although these are difficult to define and formalize.

Second, the environment calls for and allows self-management and planning by the children; provides them with a succession of tasks that require increasing persistence, patience, and attention to detail; and is responsive to small successes and gradually makes more complex demands.

Monitoring progress. In the PEP classroom, individual diagnosis and the monitoring of progress is accomplished by a combination of informal observations by the teacher, as he or she circulates among·and works with children, and the administration of criterion-referenced tests keyed to the objectives in the various structured curricula. The tests are designed for oral administration to individual children and for sampling the behaviors described in the curriculum objectives. These tests inform the teacher quite directly whether the child is or is not capable of performing the behaviors in question and involve no necessary comparison with other children or classroom norms.

Formal tests used as pretests prior to instruction assist the teacher in making instructional decisions and indicate to the child what he can expect to learn through the activities he will undertake. At the beginning of the school year, once a child is comfortable in the classroom, a test is administered to find a child's entering level in the curriculum. This test is composed of a sampling of items from various units in the curriculum, and children are rated as having mastered or not mastered certain competencies on the basis of this test. For a unit not mastered, tests on individual objectives within the unit are then administered to determine on which specific tasks the child needs to work. On the basis of this diagnosis of a child's performance, he or she is assigned appropriate activities.

While test performance usually sets the occasion for advancing to new levels in the curriculum, informal observations are most important for day-to-day teaching and diagnosis. The observations are performed as the teacher works with the children in their exploratory or prescriptive activities. These informal assessments, generally made as the child completes a prescribed task, serve to inform the teacher about the child and provide the child with a sense of competence and achievement.

Display and selection of activities. Materials for the various prescriptive curricula are arranged in color- and number-coded boxes; each box contains the materials necessary for an instructional activity. This coding permits the children to collect these materials for themselves as they work independently, with only occasional help from the teacher as needed. The activities are keyed to curriculum objectives, and typically there are several activities for each objective in order to provide for flexibility and individual choice.

To guide children's use of these materials, they are given "prescription tickets" at the beginning of each instructional session. A ticket is made up for each child daily on the basis of the teacher's observations of classroom performance and the results of recently administered tests. The tickets are displayed in the classroom on a wall chart accessible to the children. Codes on the tickets match those on the boxes so that a child can find his assigned activity and materials. The codes can be specific, directing a child to a particular activity, or they can be general, permitting the child to choose one or more of a number of activities at a given level. Thus, the child can be more or less closely directed, depending on the teacher's judgment. The prescription tickets make it possible to provide different levels of direction to different children within the same classroom.

The exploratory activities of the PEP program are open to children on a free-choice basis. The materials for these activities are displayed in the open areas of the classroom so that children can see the materials available, and observe how adults and other children use them. The tickets, hung on a special board in the classroom so that they can be taken and returned, encourage children to make a conscious decision in favor of beginning or ending an activity. A simple basis is thus provided for displaying the "rules" of the classroom and for helping children exert control over their own activities. As described earlier in this chapter, children work with a system of self-scheduling that is carefully designed so that the teacher can allow them an increasing amount of freedom of choice as they develop the capabilities for doing so.

There are typically two adults in the PEP classroom, a teacher and an aide. During an instructional period, one of the adults circulates among the children—helping with prescriptive tasks, observing how they are completed, and interacting in various ways with children in exploratory activities. These interactions are generally accomplished quite briefly. In contrast to this traveling role, the second person in the classroom works more intensively with individuals or small groups of children— administering tests, tutoring individual children, giving group lessons, or helping on a group project.

In the course of these interactions, two types of instructional functions are carried out, didactic and consultative. In the didactic role, the teacher or aide gives the various tests associated with the formal curricula, prescribes learning tasks, and checks performance on particular activities, giving help on them as required. Special tutoring sessions and large or small group lessons are also conducted as required. The consultative role is less structured and generally involves observation of the children beyond what is provided in formal testing—the use of questioning and probing techniques to stimulate reflective and problem-solving activities, helping children plan their time, and engaging in games or other activities with the children.

A Primary Grade Reading Program

The New Primary Grades Reading System (NRS) (Beck, in press; Beck & Mitroff, 1972) was specifically designed for an individualized classroom. The program permits children to progress at various rates, allows for different routes to mastery of the objectives of a lesson, and is organized so that a teacher can monitor a classroom of children doing different things at different times. Alternative teaching strategies are provided as well as opportunities for student self-direction. The program encompasses the domain traditionally carried out by the first three grades of reading instruction and is oriented toward urban children. Upon completion of the program, children are expected to be able to read and demonstrate an understanding of representative third-grade selections. Some children achieve this goal during the second year, but others may take until the fourth year.

NRS uses a code-breaking approach to beginning reading, and is organized and sequenced around grapheme/phoneme (symbol/sound) relationships and spelling patterns, thus producing initial vocabulary that emphasizes the regularity of the coding system of the English language. Instructional strategies employ both synthetic (combining sounds together) and analytic (abstracting component sounds) phonics techniques to teach children to respond to letters and strings of letters. NRS also emphasizes and rapidly introduces the meanings of words.

After a particular grapheme/phoneme correspondence is introduced, words containing that correspondence appear often in a reading context, and the text is constructed so that the child must read it and respond to its meaning. The program works back and forth in a spiral fashion between teaching new symbol/sound relationships, word attack skills, and meaning in textual materials. Early in the program, the blending of sounds to form words is given special emphasis, since it is this step that many children find difficult to accomplish. Once a repertoire of symbol/sound correspondences is acquired, the children are taught to use a blending technique, which enables them to slide sounds together to form new words. Mastery of this perform- ance enables children to attack new words independently when they contain combinations of learned symbol/sound correspond- ences. (See Chapter 6 for a discussion of NRS's blending pro- cedure.)

Instructional Resources

The NRS program is comprised of 14 levels, each containing about 10 instructional sequences or lessons. Instruction in the first two levels is conducted by the teacher with small groups of children. Starting with the third level, cassette audio tapes that children can operate independently are used for introducing new lessons. These audio lessons are a key device for individualizing instruction with beginning readers.

In NRS, there is a variety of components—prescriptive and structured; informal; child selected; and choice activities, which are additional reading experiences the child may or may not do. The central prescriptive component of NRS is the workbook, which either contains the resources needed by both teacher and child or initiates the use of other resources. The workbooks con- tain the following:

(a) Lesson overviews that outline the content of each lesson and alert the teacher to aspects of the content that should be stressed. While functioning in a traveling role, a teacher can glance at an overview to ascertain quickly the content on which a particular child is working. (b) Prescriptions consisting of listings of the resources available for each lesson (such as described below), which enable the teacher to make variable assignments. (c) Cassette response pages used in conjunction with lessons presented by audio-tape cassettes. The child listens to an appropriate cassette and completes these work pages by responding to the directions given. (d) Independent seatwork pages, which follow the audio lessons and provide the child with practice on newly and previously learned content by hav- ing him or her read and complete these work pages. (e) Teacher traveling notes, which are printed at the bottom of the seatwork pages and suggest teacher-student interactions relevant to the text on a particular page. (f) Progress checks, which are individually administered assessment devices that assist the teacher in deciding whether a student has sufficiently learned the lesson content to be able to go on to a new lesson or should have additional instruction on the content of the present lesson. (g) Group story reminders that assist the teacher in assembling a group of children together to read and share interpretations of a story.

NRS also contains games, manipulative materials, story booklets, taped stories, and correlated commercial trade books at all levels of the program. The student can make a choice to perform any, all, or none of these activities. Advertisements of these activities are placed throughout each workbook so that students are reminded of the variety of storybooks, games, or similar sources that they can choose to read or play. The vocabulary used in the storybooks and games is correlated with the content of the instuctional lesson. The details of these various components of NRS are described by Beck (in press).

Prescriptive Content

Table 5.5 is a simplified representation of the content taught in the prescriptive sequences of Level 5 of NRS, a level one-third of the way through the program. The first column of Table 5.5 designates the instructional lessons contained in the level. The other columns indicate the areas of content that are taught. The table can be read across to view the content taught in any one lesson of Level 5. For example, in Lesson 9, the letter/sound correspondence *u* as in *music* is taught; the sight words *play*, *does*, and *bear* are introduced; and a comprehension format requiring students to read and respond to *where* questions is presented. This new content is presented in cassettes 5-9-A, 5-9-B, and 5-9-C and their associated workbook exercises. Following the 5-9-C sequence is a progress check that tests mastery of the new content. The 5-9-R sequence is provided for students who do not master the new content in the first three sequences of the lesson. Cassette 5-9-D and its associated workbook exercises introduce the -*er* ending and two concepts associated with it: (a) the -*er* as used to contrast two people or objects, as in *Nan is taller than Ben*; and (b) the -*er* that is used to identify a person who does a specific action, as in

Table 5.5
Content of Prescriptive Sequences of Level 5 of NRS

Lesson	Letter/Sound Correspondences	Sight Words	Comprehension Formats	Cassette-Led Lesson Plans and Progress Checks	Group Stories	Other
1	v-v̲est	we be	Who. . . ? (Read and respond to questions asking who did something.)	5-1-A and Workbook Exercises 5-1-B and Workbook Exercises Progress Check 5-1 5-1-R and Workbook Exercises Progress Check 5-1-R		
2	plural ending es- dish̲e̲s̲	wash come your tomorrow house don't		5-2-A and Workbook Exercises 5-2-B and Workbook Exercises Progress Check 5-2 5-2-R and Workbook Exercises Progress Check 5-2-R		
3	th- ba̲t̲h̲	oh look good too	What. . . ? (Read and respond to questions asking what happened.)	5-3-A and Workbook Exercises 5-3-B and Workbook Exercises Progress Check 5-3 5-3-R and Workbook Exercises Progress Check 5-3-R		
4	ar- f̲a̲rm		When. . . ? (Read and respond to questions asking when something happened.)	5-4-A and Workbook Exercises 5-4-B and Workbook Exercises 5-4-C and Workbook Exercises Progress Check 5-4 5-4-R and Workbook Exercises Progress Check 5-4-R		
5	y- tr̲y̲			5-5-A and Workbook Exercises 5-5-B and Workbook Exercises 5-5-C and Workbook Exercises Progress Check 5-5 5-5-R and Workbook Exercises Progress Check 5-5-R		
6					Group Story: Three Wishes	
7	ō- rō̲de̸	put		5-7-A and Workbook Exercises 5-7-B and Workbook Exercises 5-7-C and Workbook Exercises Progress Check 5-7 5-7-R and Workbook Exercises Progress Check 5-7-R		
8	er- he̲r ur- hu̲rt ir- sti̲r̲	water person began		5-8-A and Workbook Exercises 5-8-B and Workbook Exercises 5-8-C and Workbook Exercises Progress Check 5-8 5-8-R and Workbook Exercises Progress Check 5-8-R		
9	ū- mū̲sic	play does bear	Where. . . ? (Read and respond to questions asking where something is.)	5-9-A and Workbook Exercises 5-9-B and Workbook Exercises 5-9-C and Workbook Exercises Progress Check 5-9 5-9-R and Workbook Exercises Progress Check 5-9-R 5-9-D and Workbook Exercises		5-9-D establishes two -er concepts, e.g., 1) Nan is taller than Ben. 2) A person who swims is a swimmer.
10					Group Story: A Time̸ to Cry	

A person who swims is a swimmer. The content of the lessons in Level 5 can now be discussed in somewhat more detail.

The selection of the specific *letter/sound correspondences* to be taught and the ordering of those correspondences in the program are major tasks in designing a decoding-based reading system. In selecting and ordering the graphemes for NRS, three guidelines are employed:

(a) Graphemes are presented relative to the ease with which the letter/sound correspondences can be learned. (b) Graphemes are presented in the order of their usefulness in combination with other known letter/sound correspondences in generating meaningful words for students. (c) Especially in the early levels, visually or aurally competitive graphemes are separated as widely as possible.

Note in Table 5.5 that in the new graphemes presented in Lessons 7 and 9, diacritical markings are placed with certain letters (i.e., rōdé, mūsic). This is done in NRS to differentiate the long-vowel sounds from the short-vowel sounds and to indicate silent letters. The diacritical markings are removed in carefully sequenced lessons approximately halfway through NRS.

It is not apparent from Table 5.5, but from the beginning levels of NRS, the new letter/sound correspondences are taught in beginning, medial, and ending positions within words if possible. For example, in Lesson 4 of Level 5, the grapheme *ar* is introduced and is used in that lesson in words such as *arm, garden,* and *car.* In Lesson 8, three graphemes that produce the same phoneme, *er* (as in *her, ur* as in *hurt,* and *ir* as in *stir*), are introduced together. This occurs occasionally in beginning levels of NRS and with increasing frequency in the upper levels.

Sight words are words that are taught as whole units. There are 19 sight words introduced in Level 5. NRS follows two general rules in introducing sight words. They are introduced when they become necessary to generate a new sentence structure, or they are introduced at a place where they can be used in a supportive, meaningful context. In general, the sight words introduced are of this latter type.

The term *comprehension formats* refers to presentation schemes located in the students' workbooks. Comprehension formats are so named because the responses required can be made only if the student has read and "understood" some of the printed text. Four new comprehension formats are introduced in Level 5, and all require that the student read a question introduced by *who, what, when,* or *where,* and then respond by selecting the appropriate multiple-choice answer.

The column entitled *Cassette-Led Lesson Plans and Progress Checks* illustrates the different ways lessons are structured in NRS. Lessons have a varying number of cassettes and sets of corresponding workbook pages, depending upon the degree of difficulty and amount of content presented in the lesson. As indicated, progress checks test the mastery of the new content.

Group Stories are regularly scheduled stories that are read and discussed by a small group of students in a teacher-led situation. In general, the instructional purposes of group stories are for the teacher to assist children with increasingly complex syntax, polysyllabic words, word meanings, and story-line development. The group story situations, however, are also important for social reasons in that they provide an opportunity for sustained peer contact and teacher-student contact. Lessons 6 and 10 of Level 5 are group stories.

The last column in Table 5.5 refers to additional content introduced throughout NRS, such as spelling patterns, homonyms, compound words, contractions, punctuation, and recognizing the actor and action in a sentence. In Level 5, the only relevant additional content is the *-er* ending.

Instructional Flow

A flow chart indicating how resources of NRS are generally used in a lesson is shown in Figure 5.6. The chart indicates that both teacher and students have decision-making opportunities to determine what should be done at various parts of the lesson. The child begins with the prescriptive components and works through cassette-led instruction, completes the relevant workbook exercises, and then has the teacher check his progress. If his performance is satisfactory, he has the choice of immediately going on to the next lesson or selecting certain choice activities before going on. If his performance on the progress checks is not satisfactory, further instruction is prescribed; generally, this

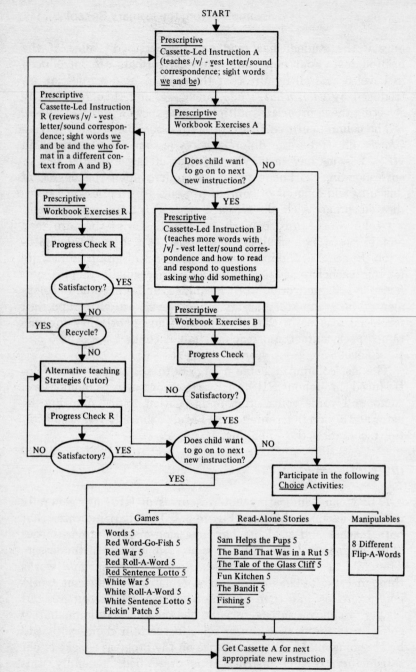

START

Prescriptive
Cassette-Led Instruction A
(teaches /v/ - vest letter/sound
correspondence; sight words
we and be)

Prescriptive
Workbook Exercises A

Does child want
to go on to next
new instruction?   NO

YES

Prescriptive
Cassette-Led Instruction
R (reviews /v/ - vest
letter/sound correspon-
dence; sight words we
and be and the who for-
mat in a different con-
text from A and B)

Prescriptive
Workbook Exercises R

Progress Check R

Satisfactory?   YES

NO

YES   Recycle?

NO

Alternative teaching
Strategies (tutor)

Progress Check R

NO   Satisfactory?   YES

Prescriptive
Cassette-Led Instruction B
(teaches more words with
/v/ - vest letter/sound correspondence and how to read
and respond to questions
asking who did something)

Prescriptive
Workbook Exercises B

Progress Check

NO   Satisfactory?

YES

Does child want
to go on to next
new instruction?   NO

YES

Participate in the following
Choice Activities:

Games	Read-Alone Stories	Manipulables
Words 5	Sam Helps the Pups 5	8 Different
Red Word-Go-Fish 5	The Band That Was in a Rut 5	Flip-A-Words
Red War 5	The Tale of the Glass Cliff 5	
Red Roll-A-Word 5	Fun Kitchen 5	
Red Sentence Lotto 5	The Bandit 5	
White War 5	Fishing 5	
White Roll-A-Word 5		
White Sentence Lotto 5		
Pickin' Patch 5		

Get Cassette A for next
appropriate new instruction

Figure 5.6. Configuration of an individualized NRS lesson (Level 5, Lesson 1).

new instruction repeats the content of the lesson in a new context.

The length of any prescriptive assignment depends upon the teacher's assessments of the student's capabilities. The use of choice activities is encouraged by the teacher, since they reinforce the content presented in the prescriptive portion of the lesson, but the particular choice of activities is usually left to the discretion of the student. The combination of choice components with prescriptive components permits a child's decisions to determine the rate at which he or she completes the program. A child who quickly learns the content of new lessons, for example, may spend time in a program because he chooses to participate in many choice activities; a child who learns less quickly may spend more time because he requires additional prescribed instruction. Futhermore, this combination presents the child with three real-life situations: having to read something at certain times, selecting one thing rather than another to read, and choosing not to read at certain times.

An Elementary School Science Program

Individualized Science (IS) is a program in the biological and physical sciences designed to serve children in grades K through 8 (Champagne & Klopfer, 1974; Klopfer, 1971). The general goals of IS include:

(a) Scientific literacy (i.e., an understanding of certain important scientific concepts and principles), the ability to use a basic scientific vocabulary to describe observations and experiences, and the understanding that scientific ideas change over time and are related to social contexts. (b) Skill in using the processes of scientific inquiry to carry out investigations of natural phenomena or problems outside of science. (c) Informed attitudes toward the study of science and the process of scientific inquiry, including a "scientific attitude" toward confronting problems—open-mindedness, suspended judgment, self-criticism, and commitment to accuracy.

In addition, the IS program attempts to develop abilities for student self-evaluation and self-direction by providing procedures for children to plan their own activities, to manage their own instructional materials, to take part in the assessment of their learning, and to select from alternate resources and units of science content.

Content and Components

At the early levels of the IS curriculum, the emphasis is on the introduction of the processes of inquiry (e.g., sorting, observing, classifying, and measuring), and the student is provided with opportunities to practice and utilize these skills while exploring a variety of science areas. At the later levels, the process of scientific inquiry is emphasized, and the students are given opportunities to carry out investigations in a problem-solving context. At the same time, they are introduced to a wide range of concepts to foster understanding and knowledge about the human as a biological system and the environment. Techniques and procedures for managing the IS materials and for self-evaluation are introduced early in the program, and students are increasingly expected and able to manage and evaluate their progress through the curriculum.

The content of IS is organized into seven levels (A through G), each of which is designed to provide an average student with one school year's experience in science. Each level consists of a number of units, which explore different science topics and which are named for a scientist whose work is related to the topic of the unit. Every unit in the program has an audio-tape filmstrip, which tells about the life and work of the scientist for whom the unit is named.

Table 5.6 lists the name and topic of each unit in the program. The units listed in the first column are "mainstream units," which comprise the basic science core that each student is expected to study and master. Before moving to the next higher level of the program, the student must be able to demonstrate competence in the objectives of the mainstream units. Beginning at Level D, there are "alternative pathway units," listed in the second column, that a student can elect to study. While the topics of the various units are discrete, certain major concepts of science are developed and recur as themes in units from level to level; these themes are biological adaptation (introduced in the Burbank unit), energy (introduced formally in the Lavoisier unit), kinetic-molecular theory (introduced very

Table 5.6

Mainstream and Alternate Pathway Units in Individualized Science

Mainstream Units	Alternative Pathway Units *
Level A	
Simpson (sorting)	
Galileo (observing)	
Michelson (measuring)	
Level B	
Burbank (classifying)	
Hooke (forces)	
Curie (physical states)	
Level C	
Lagrange (metric measurement)	
Vesalius (systems)	
Black (chemical systems)	
Level D	
Lavoisier (burning)	
Dalton (atoms and molecules)	
Haldane (breathing)	
Selected Alternative Pathway Unit	Comstock (plants and animals)
Level E	Linnaeus (plant growth)
Joule (energy)	
Beaumont (digestion)	
Voit (nutrition)	Volta (electricity)
Selected Alternative Pathway Unit	Archimedes (machines)
Level F	
Harvey (circulation)	Copernicus (solar system)
Powell (water)	
Selected Alternative Pathway Unit	Lyell (geology)
Level G	
Borelli (motion)	Siebert (microorganisms and disease)
Quetelet (variation)	
Selected Alternative Pathway Unit	Arrhenius (chemical solutions)

* Alternative Pathway Units are optional explorations which are available to the student beginning at Level D.

Note. Adapted from "An Individualized Elementary School Science Program" by A. B. Champagne and L. E. Klopfer, Theory into Practice, 1974, 13, 136-148.

simply in the Curie unit), and systems (introduced in the Vesalius unit).

Within each unit, there is a variety of modular resources for learning. These resources are designed to provide opportunities both for self-instruction and for children to learn together. A basic module is the "miniature exploration" (MinEx) consisting of illustrated booklets, manipulative materials, and cassette tapes. These impart information to students and provide them with opportunities to investigate scientific questions, to use scientific apparatus, and to carry out models of scientific exploration. Also included in the curriculum materials are suggestions for "readings in science" (RIS), teacher- or peer-led discussions, "student activities" (SA), and "science learning games" (SLG), as well as devices for keeping a plan of work, for checking on the adequacy of one's work, and for keeping a personal science notebook. Every student does not necessarily take all lessons in a unit, but takes only those that are required or which he or she has chosen to do. Lessons can be omitted if prior knowledge is demonstrated, and the resources in a unit can be used in diverse ways.

Sequence of Activities

Consider Level E in Table 5.6 as an example (see Champagne & Klopfer, 1975). The general topic of the mainstream units in Level E is energy. In the Joule unit, the student is introduced to the concepts of energy and is given examples of energy conversions in various physical systems. The Beaumont and Voit units emphasize biological systems, and focus on digestion and nutrition, respectively. In the Beaumont unit, the student studies how energy is released in the biological system of his or her own body. The student studies the physical and chemical changes in the digestive system, and then learns how end products of digestion interact with oxygen in body cells to release energy. The ways in which the body utilizes energy that is released in cells are emphasized in the Voit unit. The student also learns about the essential nutrients that provide a well-balanced diet.

Level E mainstream units introduce more quantitative techniques than do the previous levels. The student calculates heat energy in kilocalories and measures the caloric content of various quantities of foods. He or she also works with and interprets fairly complex tables and charts. The miniature explorations at this level offer the student a choice of either following a suggested plan or devising his or her own plan for answering a given question. Additional investigations are proposed to encourage the student to design and carry out his or her own procedures for conducting these investigations.

The alternative pathway units provide the student with an opportunity to expand his understanding of a topic related to the content of the mainstream or to investigate another area that may be of interest to him; these units contain many built-in choices and offer various possibilities for self-directed work and topics for independent inquiry. The Level E filmstrips on "men and ideas" consider, among other issues, the influence of the industrial revolution on Joule's study of energy and the ethics of using humans for scientific research, as in Beaumont's studies.

A planning booklet, by its design, provides a means to help the student decide in what order he or she should do the activities. Figure 5.7 shows the four pages of the planning booklet. Page 1 shows the introductory sequence; page 2, the four learning segments; page 3, the MinEx's, RIS's, and SA's; and page 4, the final activities (the seminar lesson, the posttest, and the last teacher-student conference). Notes on each page help the student make decisions about his or her sequence of activities. For example, the student is told that he may do the learning segments on page 2 after he has completed the introductory sequence, do the activities on page 3 of the booklet at any time, and that when he completes all these activities, he should go on to the activities on page 4. The student schedules a conference with the teacher to discuss preliminary plans that he or she has designed. At that time, suggestions can be made for its improvement. The short teacher-student conference helps to assess the student's progress and provides guidance for further selection of learning activities.

Figure 5.7, three pages from an IS planning booklet, shows how one student planned his activities and this record was described by Champagne and Klopfer (1975):

Eddie Biello began the Joule unit with a Teacher-Student Conference. During the conference, his teacher explained to Eddie that he would learn about energy in this unit; he would learn that there are different forms of energy, that energy can change things, and how energy changes from one form to another. Eddie's teacher told him that he should read the Placement Test and decide whether

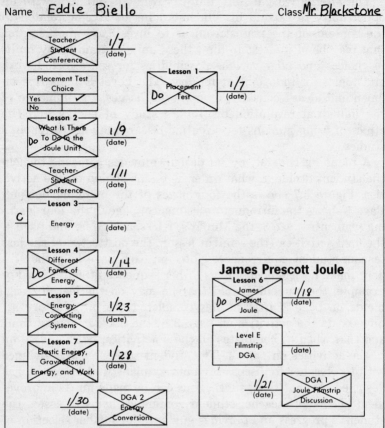

When you have finished the activities on this page, go on to page 2. Remember, you can do the activities on page 3 at any time. You can do lesson 6 any time after your second Teacher-Student Conference.

1

Figure 5.7. Joule Planning Booklet of the Individualized Science Program.

or not to do it. He added that if Eddie decided not to do it, he would have to do all the lessons. Eddie recorded the conference in his Planning Booklet. . . .

You can do any of these activities first.

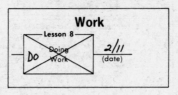

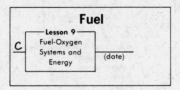

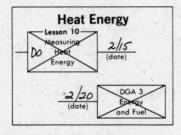

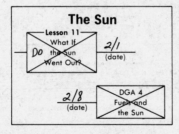

Figure 5.7. (continued) Joule Planning Booklet of the Individualized Science program.

Following the conference, Eddie did read lesson 1, the Placement Test. Eddie wanted to see how much he already knew about energy, so he elected to do the Placement Test. In lesson 2, Eddie checked his Placement Test and, by analyzing the results, he discovered that he did not have to do lessons 3 and 9. Eddie wrote "C" (for choice) on the short line next to the boxes for these two lessons. He also chose which MinEx's, SA's and RIS's he thought he would like to do and marked these in his Planning Booklet.

Other activities about:	You can do these activities at any time.	Date:
Forms of Energy	☐ MinEx 1 Can Light Energy Change Things?	
	☑ MinEx 2 Is Sound a Kind of Kinetic Energy?	1/16
	☑ MinEx 3 How Can You Make a System To Convert Heat Energy Into Kinetic Energy?	1/16
	☐ MinEx 4 How Can You Make a System To Convert Stored Gravitational Energy to Kinetic Energy?	
	☑ MinEx 5 How Can You Make a System To Convert Electrical Energy to Magnetic Energy?	1/23
	☐ MinEx 6 How Can You Make a System To Convert Stored Chemical Energy to Electrical Energy?	
	☐ SA 1 Batteries	
	☐ SA 2 Elastic Energy	
	☐ SA 3 Can You Show That Energy Has Mass or Occupies Space?	
	☐ SA 4 Community Electricity	
	☐ SA 8 Elastic Energy Machine	
	☑ SA 9 Energy Conversions	1/25
	☐ SA 12 Observing Sound	
	☐ SA 13 Paper Cup Telephone	
	☑ SA 14 Radiometer	1/25
	☑ RIS 1 A Chemical System	1/11
	☑ RIS 2 Fireflies	1/11
	☐ RIS 3 Gravity	
Work	☑ SA 6 Gravitational Energy	2/13
Fuel	☐ SA 5 Fuels	
Heat Energy	☑ MinEx 7 How Can You Make a System To Convert Electrical Energy to Heat Energy?	2/20
	☐ MinEx 8 How Can You Measure Heat Energy?	
	☑ SA 10 What Happens When You Add the Same Amount of Heat Energy to Equal Masses of Salt and Water?	2/18
	☐ SA 11 How Is Heat Energy Measured?	
	☐ SA 15 Energy Game	
	☐ SA 16 Energy Solitaire	
	☑ RIS 6 Calories	2/18
The Sun	☑ SA 7 Solar Energy	2/4
	☐ RIS 4 Nuclear Energy	
	☑ RIS 5 How Does the Sun Get Its Energy?	2/4
	☐ RIS 7 Conservation of Energy	
"How To . . ." Booklets	You can find out more about doing science activities by reading "How To . . ." booklets. Some of the booklets are: How To . . .	

Do SA's   Answer Questions and Check Your
Do RIS's   Answers
Do MinEx's   Use Your Science Notebook
Do SIIA's   Treat Burns
Use an Alternative   Use Glass Safely
   Pathway Unit   Use Chemicals Safely

Figure 5.7. (continued) Joule Planning Booklet of the Individualized Science program.

When Eddie went to see his teacher for the second Teacher-Student Conference, his teacher was busy. Eddie decided to do an RIS while he waited. In fact, he did RIS 1 and RIS 2 and then met with his teacher to go over the test results and to discuss his plan for working through the unit.

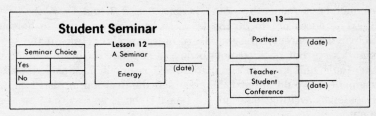

Record SIIA's, SLG's, "How To . . ." booklets, and books you read here. If you do SA's from
other Level E units, record them here, too.

SIIA - How Does a Dam Convert Water Power to
Electrical Energy?

KEY	
MinEx	= Miniature Exploration
SA	= Student Activity
RIS	= Readings in Science
DGA	= Directed Group Activity
SIIA	= Self-Initiated Independent Activity
SLG	= Science Learning Game

Figure 5.7. (continued) Joule Planning Booklet of the Individualized Science program.

Note. From "Level E Teacher's Manual, Individualized Science" by A. B. Champagne
and L. E. Klopfer (Kankakee, Ill.: Imperial International Learning Corp., 1975).

Before Eddie could go on to the learning segments, he had to
complete the introductory sequence. Because he did not have to do
lesson 3, he began with lesson 4. He decided he wanted to do lesson
6 next. Eddie met with his teacher to plan when he could do the
related DGA 1. While waiting for some other classmates to participate in the DGA, he did two MinEx's. Eddie completed the in-

troductory sequence by doing lessons 5 and 7 and DGA 2.

Eddie chose not to do the learning segment on Fuel, so he participated in three of the four learning segments. (He read the seminar lesson, but decided not to do the seminar during his work in the Joule unit.) As he completed each segment, he decided which segment he would do next. He recorded the decision in his Planning Booklet by writing "Do" in the box for the lesson in the new segment.

Let's take a brief look at Eddie's progress in just one of the learning segments, "The Sun." He began his work in the segment with lesson 11 and did well. Eddie decided he wanted to do SA 7 and RIS 5, two activities related to the content of lesson 11. On the next science day, he did the activities and recorded the date next to their names on page 3 of his Planning Booklet. The next activity indicated in his Planning Booklet was DGA 4. Eddie met with his teacher to discuss his progress and to schedule a day on which to do the DGA. He asked his teacher for some advice on an SIIA he had thought about. Eddie worked on the SIIA until it was time for the DGA. After he completed DGA 4 and his SIIA, Eddie felt that he had finished the learning segment on energy from the sun. (pp. 35–36)

Like the other programs described in this chapter, as students progress through the levels of the Individualized Science program, they learn to take more and more responsibility for the direction and evaluation of their learning. Concurrently, the number and complexity of resources for learning increase to match the increasing sophistication of the student. In IS, individual lessons are replaced by invitations to explore, which involve several concepts and combine the features of earlier lessons. Explorations increase in time from several days to a few weeks. Students begin to conduct group discussions and seminars. A similar evolution takes place in other learning resources.

General Program Characteristics

The characteristics of classroom and schoolwide systems that are responsive to individual differences undoubtedly will take many forms and incorporate new ideas as they are developed and studied. There are, however, certain characteristics of events that occur in the course of instruction under the programs that have been described in this chapter. These events can be categorized as follows:

1. *The activity of the learner guides instruction.* Student initiative is emphasized to encourage active, concentrated involvement with the environment for learning. Planning activities are gradually transformed into internal abilities of sustained self-direction that require decreasingly less support from external sources. In this self-management process, experience is provided in working with teachers and peers so that the effect of one's actions on others and on the attainment of common educational goals can be observed.

2. *Outcomes of learning are expressed in terms of observable manifestations of desired competence.* While what may be easily observed is not necessarily synonymous with desired goals of instruction, effective guidance of learning requires analysis and definition of the performance domain involved. Instruction by the teacher and learning by the students are assisted by specifying the structure of a domain of knowledge and skills in terms of its subgoal competencies and possible paths along which students can progress to acquire increasingly complex and skillful performance.

The curricula presented in this chapter emphasize the analysis of educational goals into a progressive series of subgoals through which instruction and learning proceed. The implemented structure and arrangement of these subgoals are functions of the subject matter being taught, the approach of the course designers to the subject matter, and the way in which the student elects, or his performance advises, instruction to proceed. For any particular individual, some subgoals may be omitted, added to, or combined. These subgoals provide points at which information about performance can be obtained and instructional decisions can be made.

3. *Prerequisite learning that is required for more complex learning is identified.* Two classes of learning are emphasized—specific subject-matter knowledge and skills, and generalizable cognitive and social capabilities. The instructional process is facilitated by continuous identification of the most advanced competence that a student can skillfully perform or, if a student

is unsuccessful at a particular task, by determination of the prerequisite tasks at which he is most successful. This type of upward and downward branching helps accomplish a match between the student's level of competence and the structure of the subject-matter domain. In addition, as was particularly pointed out in discussing the PEP program, the attempt is made to strengthen generalizable cognitive abilities and aptitudes that can enable the child to benefit maximally from the instructional environment.

4. *Diagnostic assessment is made of the state of the learner entering a particular instructional situation.* To be useful in instructional placement, tests and less formal observation by the teacher provide information in terms of subgoals that indicate specific knowledge and skills already mastered, partially learned, or not yet mastered by the individual learner. Thus, such assessments are referenced to particular criteria of competence. Prescriptions by the teacher or choices by the student are the result of decisions based upon adequate information.

In the early stages of a particular educational period or in the introduction to a new subject matter, instruction is adapted to the individual on the basis of initial placement information. As learning proceeds, both the teacher and the student build up information on general performance capabilities, styles of learning, and specific acquired competencies that are relevant to next immediate learning experiences.

As students learn, their performance is monitored and repeatedly assessed at longer or shorter intervals appropriate to what is being taught or to the level of learning involved. In the early stages of a subject matter, assessment is almost continuous. Later on, as competence grows, as problems grow larger, and as students become increasingly self-sustaining, assessment occurs less frequently. The information obtained from this monitoring of performance provides a basis for feedback to the learner, and is also a basis for adaptation to learner requirements.

5. *Educational alternatives are available that match the student's educational performance and attainments.* Alternate instructional procedures and materials are assigned differentially to students or made available to them for their selection. Decisions about instructional alternatives are made on the basis of teacher prescription, student selection, or some combination of

the two. In most conventional educational environments, adaptation takes place on the basis of class grouping and special work with students, where this is possible. The programs described in this chapter attempt to go beyond this and provide a more open classroom setting where increased opportunities for different instructional paths are available.

Through curriculum materials used by the teacher and the student, instructional alternatives are adaptive in various ways to the student: his present level of achievement and his retention of previous learning; his mastery of the prerequisites necessary for new learning; the speed at which he learns, including the amount of practice he requires; his ability to learn in structured prescriptive or less structured exploratory situations; his interests; and his style of work.

In general, instruction and learning proceed in an environment that provides a mutually supportive interaction between assessments of student performance, available means for learning, and standards of competence that the learning environment maintains. Beyond such communicated standards, provision always needs to be made for the ability of students to surpass expectations.

Summary

A classroom setting and various programs for developing competence in the skills and knowledge of the preschool and elementary school have been presented. Beginning work along these lines has been described elsewhere (Glaser, 1968; Lindvall & Bolvin, 1967). The author is especially familiar with these programs, having observed their development and having seen them operate in classrooms on a day-to-day basis. However, the reader is encouraged to refer to other work on individualized programs.

An up-to-date collection describing various systems of individualized education is available (Talmage, 1975). There are also examples of curricula that employ computer assistance for individualization, such as elementary reading (Atkinson, 1974; Atkinson & Hansen, 1966) and elementary mathematics (Cooley & Glaser, 1969; Suppes, Jerman, & Brian, 1968). At the college level, the individualization of instruction has been implemented by the Keller system of Personalized Instruction, a procedure that adjusts to individual progress (Keller, 1968; Sherman, 1974).

All these attempts, in varying degrees, are characterized by the properties exemplified in this chapter: observable and assessable outcomes of learning; diagnoses of learner competencies prior to instruction; alternatives for instruction that can be matched to the performance of the learner; monitoring of individual performance at relatively frequent intervals so that information is provided for instructional decisions made by the teacher, the student, or instructional device; and mutually supportive interaction between observations of student performance, means for learning, and criteria of competence.

The principles and practices that characterize the programs described in this chapter comprise a set of requirements for individualizing instruction. However, the success of any present set of principles for individualizing instruction is limited by certain constraints. Even when the operational plan is carried out well in a school setting, there are limitations of technical capability and of our knowledge about human behavior that require study. Some research and development efforts that are being carried out with respect to the study of classroom processes, the evaluation of learning outcomes, and the psychology of learning and cognition relevant to school learning are described in Chapter 6, where the need for research and development in education is considered in relation to the nature of teaching as a profession.

Chapter 6 Professionalism and Research

When love and skill work together expect a
  masterpiece.
In fine art, the heart, the head, and the hand
  go together.

J. Ruskin, circa 1860

It is important to remind ourselves that adaptive education, as
an educational pattern, has both realizable and potentially realizable aspects. Examples of realizable aspects were described in
Chapter 5. Such programs can be implemented in schools, and
their effects can be monitored and assessed to provide information for revision and improvement. Potentially realizable aspects
require research and development that can contribute to the
further development of new educational patterns. Three inter-
related research and development activities are involved:

(a) Field research focused on ongoing school programs to obtain information about the strengths and weaknesses of these
programs. (b) Developmental work concerned with the design
and implementation of new instructional procedures, curricula,
and administrative practices. (c) Laboratory research on the
cognitive and psychosocial processes of children as these processes relate to education and learning.

In this chapter, each of these three activities is discussed. As
a setting for this discussion, we consider teaching as a profession that requires active exchange between science and practice.
We argue for strengthening the teaching profession through its
increasing involvement and partnership in the study of its work.
We describe various research endeavors in order to call attention
to the importance of research as a means for informed school
change.

The Profession of Teaching

Research and development in education is related to the nature of teaching as a profession. In a 1974 issue of *American Education*, Myrtle Bonn made the observation that with respect to the professionalism of teachers, there is

a peculiarly American paradox—a paradox compounded of a high regard for education on one hand and the generally low regard that has usually been accorded teachers on the other. Time and the kind of people entering the profession have enormously elevated the status of teachers, of course, but historically they have drawn mixed reviews (p. 24).

When we consider the professional status of teachers, we should take a message from other professions in our society, such as medicine, engineering, dentistry, and law. What gives these professions status is that each involves professional skills and knowledge that are difficult to learn, and each is supported by the resources of major industries, foundations, and research organizations. Engineers and physicians, in particular, receive institutional support in the design, development, and refinement of the tools and procedures they use. An integral part of these professions are institutional structures that provide information and materials that contribute to their effectiveness and require constant new learning on the part of the members of the profession. To a large extent, a profession takes on social and monetary status because it is the recipient of technologies that its members must learn and continue to learn to carry out their functions. In comparison with these professions, teaching has not enjoyed the benefits of strong backup by research and development capabilities.

The professionalism of teaching is frequently under attack; Broudy (1972), for example, describes the pressures that converge to accelerate deprofessionalization. Individuals in all walks of life honestly believe that the only requirements for being an effective teacher are to "like children" and have a good knowledge of the subject matter; good teachers come by their talents naturally, and no special education in teaching is required. Teaching is lower in status than working with a subject matter in other ways; the folklore being "those who can, do; those who can't, teach." This folklore is currently under serious challenge at all levels of education, including the college level where, as compared with secondary and elementary levels, no training in educational technique is required.

The cry for educational reform from many quarters frequently detracts from the professionalization of teaching. Many of the proposals offered seek school innovation by bypassing the teacher training establishment rather than by seeking to improve it (e.g., employing teachers not trained in conventional ways). Activities in the development of curriculum materials, specialized testing procedures, and instrumentation for classroom teaching often are a mixed blessing to the professionalization of teaching. On the one hand, there is the implied threat of taking things out of the hands of the teacher and providing "teacher-proof" materials; on the other hand, there is the helpful attitude that teachers need good tools for their work and that technical support in building them is characteristic of most strong professions.

The provision of "teacher-proof" materials and the consequent loss of autonomy by teachers is related to another indication of the relatively low professional status of teachers. Broudy (1972) observed that, like many other large systems, school systems and the teachers in them tend to live by rules that are supposed to take care of standard cases, with only slight adjustments allowed for departures from the standard. There are, for example, rules that organize the educational continuum into grades, and for each grade there are prescriptions concerning the kinds of information and skills to be covered in the course of the school year. There are also rules about the logistics of living in the school environment, which pertain to attendance, time periods, and movement through the building.

Of course no complex system can do without certain accepted rules of conduct. What is important to observe, however, is not just the presence of rules, but an imbalance caused by a preoccupation with rules and standard procedures. This results from an imbalance between a system of rules and a set of heuristic principles that provide general guides to action and free teachers from the narrow specificity of standard operating procedures. Workbooks, manuals, and other materials for teachers frequently display "cookbook" formats, designed on the premise that teachers need and expect specific, standard operating procedures that cover most anticipated events in the classroom.

Excessively rule-ridden operations and practices attest to the lack of a teacher's professionalism. Broudy (1972) pointed out that rules frequently restrict the teacher's autonomy to trivialities; a teacher is expected to make only minor adaptations in a program of study, in instructional procedures, or in teaching style. Major changes in practice are generally not expected of teachers and are often discouraged by the school milieu. Rules become overly important to the system because there are no other strong principles of order or guides to action. The problem stems not from teachers and school systems themselves, but from the fact that a science of instruction and a set of principles derived from it are only beginning to develop as a systematic framework for educational practice.

It is generally accepted that a strong framework of theory and empirical evidence provides a basis for practice in medicine, engineering, and law, but that such a framework is lacking in education. However, applications from theory and empirical findings of the behavioral and social sciences to instructional practice are increasing in frequency. For example, recent research in perceptual learning, cognition, and language development is influencing thinking about beginning reading programs (e.g., Gibson & Levin, 1975; Resnick & Beck, 1976); developmental psychology applied to early education is influencing the design of classroom environments for young children and preschoolers (Day & Parker, in press; Kohlberg, 1968); theories of learning and memory are being applied to the design of computer-assisted instruction (e.g., Atkinson & Wilson, 1969) and to instruction that influences aptitudes and readiness skills required for further learning (e.g., Estes, 1974; Resnick & Glaser, 1976). The professional ideal involves contributing to and working toward such developments.

Scientific Knowledge and Practice

For the professionalization of teaching, it is not enough that schools of education offer courses that provide the teacher and school administrator with concepts from various disciplines and a context into which the aims of education, the curriculum, the teaching-learning process, and the organization of schools can be placed. Indeed, schools of education are very sensitive to developments in disciplines that underlie the educational process, and many exciting courses are offered. The problem with these courses, in relation to the professionalization of teaching, however, resides in the fact that they do not provide a foundation from which principles for explicit pedagogical practice can be derived in the way that principles are derived from scientific theory and empirical findings in other professional fields. On this matter, Broudy (1972) wrote the following:

> This is an issue in all general studies and in the role of foundational studies in any professional curriculum. The most plausible defense of them is to point out that they provide the *context of practice* rather than the *rules for practice*. Thus, an understanding of the sociology of poverty does not directly give rules for healing the diseases of the poor, but the dietary prescriptions that a physician might give to the poor will be more enlightened if he does understand the sociology of their condition. Knowledge of social context, therefore, affects the general strategy of education, of appraising the teaching situation in many dimensions, and for making decisions that take account of these dimensions. (pp. 56–57)

While this context-setting function of disciplinary foundations is extremely important, education also requires theory for deriving teaching methodology from disciplinary foundations. Working toward the increasing professionalization of teaching requires a conception of the relationship between science and practice which is different from the one we have generally held. Many of us were taught that progress based on science occurs through a linear sequence of events: from basic research, to applied research, to development, to practice and application. But, this conception seems to be no longer applicable, if in fact it ever was. The relation between science and progress in education is more complex, and the notion of a linear progression from basic research to application is too simplistic.

Although we take it for granted that development feeds on science, we fail to appreciate that science, in turn, attempts to solve practical problems and develop new technologies. The coupling between science and application is more reciprocal than many of us have realized. These two elements feed into and correct one another; new scientific knowledge encourages practical applications, and failures or challenges in practice often motivate fundamental science (Brooks, 1968; David, 1972).

It is this interactive mode of operation among application, development, and basic science that is to be encouraged for education. In this context, the importance of the intuitive design of sound educational practices by outstanding teachers cannot be denied. Good practice is partially based on artistry and intuition that must not be restricted, but which may be aided by attempts at analyzing and understanding the instructional process. Ideally, the job of educational research is to work within these two extremes, contributing to both knowledge and practice, and trying to understand and contribute to each without inhibiting either. This interactive mode of operation will enhance professionalization in education by breaking down the conventional standoff between academic and scientific pursuits on the one hand and professional operating concerns on the other.

Sustained cooperative ventures with a cohesive focus in which academic researchers have attempted to address educational problems and educators have solicited the help of researchers have been the exception rather than the rule. Researchers frequently have found it too easy to turn educational problems into manageable disciplinary studies that contribute to scientific knowledge, but which contribute little to the information needed to determine operating policy and courses of action. Educators, under the constraints of many pressures, have attempted innovations and improvements that have sometimes solved immediate problems, but which have not often yielded the kinds of general constructive principles required for sustained understanding of the educational process and for establishing future directions.

The objective is to bring about mutual facilitation of research and practice so that each strengthens the other. Various mechanisms and organizations devoted to this mutual facilitation need to be clarified so that the limited resources available can be used effectively to cope with the challenges that are facing education today and in the future. The professional wisdom inherent in good teaching, the carefully evaluated development of new practices, and attempts at scientific understanding must be articulated in order to develop principles of effective education and practices that implement and exemplify these principles. Sustained work along these lines will no doubt build up the professional aspects and the scientific underpinnings of education.

We alluded in Chapter 3 to the necessity for strengthening the relationships between science and practice, and in the remainder of this chapter we provide examples of the kind of research and development that we see contributing to the requirements of adaptive education, and education in general, and to increasing the professionalization of teachers.

Research in the School and the Classroom

Recent events make it urgent that teachers and school administrators become strong advocates of, and active participants in, research leading to effective school change. Highly influential, widely discussed and analyzed national surveys have suggested the relative ineffectiveness of schools to provide equality of educational opportunity and to maximize the educational achievement of our children.

We are all familiar to some degree with the Coleman (1966) and the Jencks (1972) reports, and it is not the task of this monograph to analyze the details of these studies, nor the various critiques and reactions to their accuracy and interpretation. This has already been carefully done; for example, Mayeske and his colleagues (1972) and a series of articles in the *Harvard Educational Review* (Jackson et al., 1973) discussed these controversial studies. From the point of view of our concern for school innovation, reports like these provide further impetus for the serious study of school practices. The educational community must be an active leader in such studies and must not merely take a passive or defensive stand.

In our efforts to improve the quality of our educational system, it should be kept in mind that these reports are about schooling as it generally exists; they do not consider the possibilities of new approaches to schooling, such as patterns of adaptive education with which we are concerned in this book. Jencks and his associates (1972), for example, wrote the following:

In concluding this discussion, we must again emphasize one major limitation of our findings. We have only examined the effects of resource differences among existing public schools. This tells us that if schools continue to use their resources as they now do, giving them more resources will not change children's test scores. If schools used their resources differently, however, additional resources might conceivably have larger payoffs. . . . There is no way of testing this theory except by experimentation. Past history is discouraging, but the future is not always a rerun of the past. (p. 97)

We agree, of course, that simply increasing school resources, without using them differently, is not sufficient for improving our children's education (Rivlin, 1973). We also call for experimentation in the use of school resources, as does Coleman. In commenting on the Jencks book, Coleman (1973) said:

It is also not clear from the existing data just what investment of public resources is most effective in increasing cognitive skills and level of education. What is clear is that improving "school quality" by the standard measures of quality (class size, quality of textbooks, school physical plant, teachers' experience, library size, and others) has little effect on cognitive skills. This kind of negative knowledge exists; apparently innovations in education, together with careful examination of their effects, are necessary to learn positive directions for such investment. (p. 137)

A point to be made in this regard is that reallocation of the resources over which school administrators and school boards exercise control may neither significantly influence those aspects of school life that do affect children, nor change the way teachers and students behave toward one another in their daily classroom interaction. Thus, it is important to argue for research and experimentation that is more directly related to the details of what goes on inside the classroom.

Many of the detailed aspects of the classroom have not been effectively examined in studies of the Coleman and Jencks variety. It is only with detailed information from the classroom that informed decisions can be made about the kind, amount, and allocation of resources. Furthermore, in agreement with other studies, a reanalysis of the Coleman report data (Mayeske et al., 1972) makes clear that family background measures and school resource measures are substantially intercorrelated and that most of their influence on children's achievement operates jointly. Schooling takes place in the context of families and neighborhoods, and the effects of community setting and of the nature of schooling, in combination, influence achievement. Effective investigation of the effects of schooling and of how schools might be improved must take into account the coordinated influence of these factors.

For this purpose, we advocate that continued improvement in the schools, like the continued improvement of the other services provided to improve the quality of life in our society, becomes the concern of all participants in the enterprise. School boards and school personnel, students and their families, and research and development personnel should join as partners in bringing about educational improvement and reform—reform that is based not on meaningless slogans or political platforms, but upon innovations that are tried out and carefully studied in schools. In this process, teachers and school administrators should be the prime movers and catalytic agents for action. Particularly, it is necessary to go beyond looking at global school resources, as has been done in large survey studies, and to examine classroom processes in detail.

Teachers and school administrators need to work with researchers in the study of day-to-day interactions in the classroom. Such detailed analyses of the instructional process should enable us to identify effective practices as they occur in the context of particular school environments with particular school populations. It is the investigation of these details that provides the information necessary for determining the effectiveness of new educational patterns and for suggesting ways in which they can be improved. Research models for this purpose are available (e.g., Cooley & Emrick, 1974; Cooley & Leinhardt, 1975; Cooley & Lohnes, 1976; Stallings & Kaskowitz, 1974), and we now turn to considerations of one such model.

Studying Classroom Processes

Components of classroom processes are particuarly important to observe and study in order to understand what influences educational outcomes. All too frequently, educational reports present detailed data on initial student performance and criterion performance measures, but give only broad-brush information about actual classroom practices and procedures—

information that could provide a strong basis for understanding the strengths and weaknesses of particular instructional programs. The need for information about classroom processes is especially great when a school system adopts a new curriculum or a new pattern of teaching. The new method is generally compared with methods that have been used in the past so that a decision can be made about adoption and dissemination of the new program. In many situations of this kind, what is frequently neglected is the way in which the innovation under consideration is actually implemented by teachers and students in the classroom.

Some teachers may carry out the new practices as intended by the curriculum developer; some teachers may grasp the principles underlying the innovation, and improve on or adapt the specific recommended practices to local requirements; other teachers may actively resist the innovation by using the new materials together with practices they have used for years because they are comfortable doing what they know how to do best. Without knowledge of what actually occurs in the classroom, it is impossible to adequately assess the effects of changes and to provide teachers and school administrators with the kind of information they require for continued improvement of their efforts.

One framework for conceptualizing research on the effects of changes in instructional practice that has been developed is designed to explain the variation in student performance that occurs among classrooms following an extended period of instruction (Cooley & Lohnes, 1976). Figure 6.1 illustrates the elements of the general framework. Three main categories are considered: criterion performance—achievement and educational outcomes; initial student performance—readiness skills, aptitude, learning style, general knowledge and skill; and between these two, various components of the processes that characterize classroom practices.

Criterion performance refers to the educational outcomes that are expressed as the goals of an educational system. In the elementary school, these include learning basic skills and knowledge (academic achievement); self-esteem and feelings of self-worth and self-control; the ability to understand and feel comfortable with others who are different from one's self in various ways; positive attitudes and interest toward school and

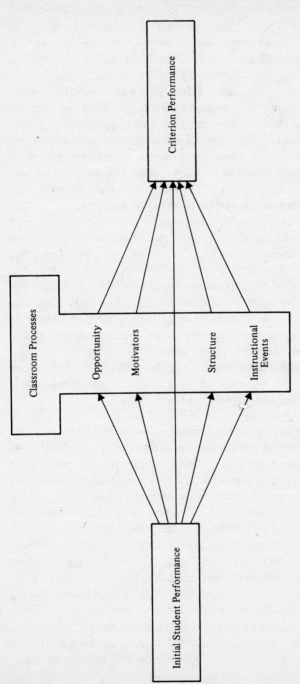

Figure 6.1. Cooley-Lohnes model of classroom processes.
Note. Adapted from Evaluation Research in Education by W. W.
Cooley and P. R. Lohnes (New York: Irvington Publishers, 1976).

learning; creativity of expression and the ability to question ideas, enjoyment, and appreciation of the cultural accomplishments of society; and a sense of citizenship and community in society.

Initial student performance refers to what we earlier called "entering competence." It relates to aspects of behavior that a student brings into the classroom and which influence learning. As we have indicated, initial student performance is predictive of criterion performance, and accounts for a significant portion of the achievement outcomes in schools and classrooms. These initial student abilities also comprise an important basis for instruction and are influenced by classroom practices.

In analyzing the effects of classroom practices, it is important to study the extent to which differences in school outcome performance are influenced by initial abilities, by classroom practices, or by the interaction between the two. While evidence makes it clear that school outcomes are related to measured intelligence, socioeconomic status, and similar variables, the problem for school improvement is to determine the extent to which classroom practices can capitalize upon, strengthen, and in other ways take account of and adapt to entering competence.

Classroom processes are described (see Figure 6.1) in terms of four components representing operational characteristics of classroom practices (Cooley & Leinhardt, 1975).

1. *Opportunity* refers to the extent to which the kind of learning that takes place in the classroom is represented in the assessments of criterion performance. In particular, opportunity refers both to the amount of time spent by the student or scheduled by the teacher in a particular subject matter, and to the extent to which the materials sampled in measures of criterion performance are actually covered in classroom activities.

With respect to time, teachers in different classrooms may permit children to work on a subject matter for different amounts of time, and one would expect that students who have a 90-minute period to work on mathematics, for example, would learn more than students allotted only a 45-minute period.

With respect to the extent of coverage, in certain classrooms the curriculum materials may overlap a good deal with what is covered in end-of-year achievement tests, whereas in other classrooms the teacher might spend more time on topics not sampled by the test. In assessing this component of classroom processes, information needs to be provided about the amount of time available for and actually spent by students in various subject-matter areas. Also important to determine is the relationship between what is taught in the classroom and the end-of-year assessment of student outcomes.

2. *Motivators* refer to two complex sets of events. First, they refer to the behaviors and attitudes that a student brings to the classroom and which support attention to learning and high rates of learning activity. Second, they refer to those aspects of the educational environment that increase the likelihood of an individual's engaging in sustained learning activities when the opportunity is present.

The motivator component of the model is concerned with these latter aspects, and consists of observable features of the classroom environment that are designed to encourage the student to undertake learning activity. Motivators include a variety of events, such as teacher reinforcement for attending to work, the opportunity for peer interaction, and interesting instructional materials and activities. Available curriculum materials may be uniformly dull as compared with curricula that allow teachers to introduce varied and interesting activities. The teacher's interpersonal interaction with students can be more or less motivating as a result of the particular ways in which a teacher encourages independent student work, asks questions, and attends to student instructional requirements. Peer interaction, generally assumed to be motivating to students, can be either useful or wasteful, depending on the details of its application and organization. Teacher sensitivity to the student's cultural background can influence motivation; some students look for strong authority, while others require more of a partnership, especially in the beginning of a school year before the teacher's particular style and expectations have been established.

3. *Structure* refers to the way in which a curriculum is organized and sequenced. The clarity and specificity of the objectives of instruction may be more or less obvious and defined; the sequence may be linear and provide few points at which students can branch to new instructional options, or it may provide many branching points to allow differential student progress. If branch-

ing options are provided, then learning activities can be matched to various student requirements, including student interest, progress, and learning style. Performance on tests that are integrally keyed to instructional materials can provide suggestions for learning activities.

Various combinations of student, teacher, and curriculum-specified instructional decisions can assist in matching student abilities to instructional activities, and this matching can be done more or less accurately. Matching may take place frequently or infrequently, and it may involve the class as a whole, a smaller group of children, or one child.

4. *Instructional events* refer to interaction of an instructional nature between student and teacher, or among students. In particular, this component of classroom processes is concerned with the content, quality, duration, and frequency of interpersonal interactions. A series of questions is illustrative:

What is the content of a teacher's interaction with a student? Is it concerned with the subject matter being learned? Is it an explanation of how to use and manage instructional materials? How does the teacher go about explaining things? How one-sided is the interaction? How much opportunity is there for the student to respond, to indicate his or her knowledge, or to ask questions? What is the emotional tone of the interaction? Is it positive, or negative and punitive? In general, how much student contact and personal interaction does the classroom setting allow? How perceptive is the teacher in focusing on the student's requirements for learning?

The study of classroom processes as described in this section can impinge directly on the teacher's professional freedom. In order to learn from information about the influence and effects of their work, teachers must open up their classes for observation. This is difficult to do because one does not necessarily enjoy being under detailed observation unless one is either especially secure or very cavalier about one's working activities. However, if teachers participate as partners in the study of their activities toward the objective of professional improvement, then situations requiring observational study will be less threatening.

What is obtained from classroom study is information. For the teacher, it is not the information itself that is threatening, but how the information is used. The results of classroom research should become a source for discussion and feedback about how teaching activities might be changed or continued. The information obtained need not necessarily provide a basis for the evaluation of individual worth. Just as diagnostic tests given to students can be used as supportive information for making informed instructional decisions, classroom data can be used without raising the threat of "grading." Effective practice requires indicators and information, and the study of classroom processes should be seen in this light by the teachers and administrators in schools.

Development of Curriculum Materials and Procedures

In recent years, a growing amount of activity has been concerned with systematic procedures for the development of curriculum materials, instructional procedures, and classroom administrative practices. As noted earlier in this chapter, one sign of a strong profession is the amount of resources and the quality of activity devoted to the development of professional tools to be used by the practitioner and the client. In this regard, the aspect of educational practice that has received major research and development support has been the technology of testing. A sizable industry exists that provides testing materials to the education profession.

The use of tests as tools of the profession has also been institutionalized in schools of education through the existence of required courses in tests and measurements. In their professional education, teachers are exposed to fundamental concepts of test development and use, such as validity, reliability, standardization, and interpretation of scores. Less emphasized in teacher education are courses on the fundamentals of the design of instruction that can assist teachers in making informed judgments about educational materials. This omission is no doubt a result of the fact that the explicit statement of principles of instructional design is a recent event.

However, many recent books and articles reflect a trend toward the systematic design of instruction (Gagné & Briggs, 1974; Gow, 1976; Holland, Solomon, Doran, & Frezza, 1976; Merrill, 1971; Popham & Baker, 1970a, 1970b, 1970c; Resnick,

1975). Instructional design is becoming part of formal courses in schools of education, and developers and publishers of educational materials are also beginning to incorporate these principles in their work. This new emphasis is obviously important to the theme of this monograph which is concerned with the design and development of adaptive instructional systems.

Educational practitioners become significant participants in this effort by contributing to the development and tryout of new materials and practices in their classrooms and by making well-founded decisions about the selection of materials for school use. The development of an instructional program is obviously a complex and time-consuming matter, and for the many necessary details involved, the reader is referred to the references given above.

Table 6.1 provides a brief summary of the steps required for the development of instructional materials and procedures. Ten steps are described in this table, beginning with the analysis and identification of instructional needs, continuing through the development and testing of instructional materials, the design of classroom procedures, and evaluation and operational implementation. Of particular significance in this work is the planned recycling, whereby program components undergo tryout, assessment, and modification over a number of iterations before the end product is ready for full school implementation. The curriculum development process outlined in this table occurs over a period of years. Our experience suggests, for example, that a kindergarten through grade 3 reading program would take about five years from conception to availability.

Research on the Psychology of Learning and Cognition

So far, we have discussed two areas of research. The first, field research in schools, is concerned with investigation of classroom settings, and of how the characteristics of students and specific classroom practices affect instructional outcomes. The second, development of materials and practices, is concerned with the design, construction, and testing of tools to be used by teachers and students for teaching and learning. We turn now to a third area, more removed from the classroom than the first two, but nevertheless requiring the understanding of teachers and stu-

Table 6.1

Steps in the Development of an Instructional Program

1. Analysis and identification of needs. The design of an instructional program results from some perceived need. With respect to school curricula, this can include the need to conduct instruction more effectively and efficiently, to update the content and teaching methods of some existing course, or to develop a new course.

2. Definition of goals and objectives. The knowledge and skills that are to be the outcomes of the instructional program are specified. The terminal objectives are analyzed into subobjectives, and their common elements, prerequisite relations, and possible learning difficulties are identified.

3. Design of assessment procedures. This step involves the preparation of tests, observation schedules, and other means of measuring student performance, the feasibility and effectiveness of instruction, and the attainment of instructional objectives. The design of assessment procedures helps to further specify goals and objectives and provides measures to be used in subsequent stages.

4. Formulation of instructional strategies and the properties of the learning environment. The kinds of behavior and cognitive performances that comprise the objectives of the instructional program are analyzed in terms of what is known about how they are learned in relation to the nature of the students and their entering capabilities. Required resources are considered, including teaching staff and assistants, various kinds of media, and classroom structure.

5. Development and preliminary testing of instructional materials. Initial lesson designs are constructed and tested by the teacher and the lesson designer, working with a few children from the target population. The information obtained is used to review the adequacy of the initial specification of objectives, instructional sequences, and teaching strategies, and to revise instructional materials and procedures.

6. Design of the educational environment and management procedures. The spatial layout of classroom areas, the location of materials, and the flow of students among these areas are considered. The teacher behaviors necessary for the implementation and conduct of the new program are identified.

7. Preparation of teacher training materials and conduct of training programs. Materials development and teacher training can be carried out in conjunction with one another, with teachers being involved at various points to assist in development, to become familiar with the program, and to make suggestions for its implementation.

8. Field tryouts, formative evaluation, and revision. The program is implemented on a small scale to observe its operation and effects. The objective is to obtain information on many aspects of the program in order to revise and improve them. This work is generally carried out in a series of stages with various components of the program until the entire program has been tested and revised.

9. Field testing, collection of data, and reporting of program characteristics and effectiveness. The full-scale program is implemented in one or more schools with the population for which it was designed. An appropriate evaluation plan is instituted so that information is obtained about the strengths and weaknesses of the program.

10. Operational implementation and dissemination. If expectations for the success of the program are met, it is ready for adoption and regular use. The results of wide-scale adoption are analyzed to provide information for adjustments to local requirements. A program of quality control for continued monitoring of the use and effectiveness of the program is instituted.

dents who may frequently become participants in this work. This third area concerns research on the psychology of learning, and on the cognitive processes that underlie the acquisition of the knowledge and competencies learned in school. (For a general review, see Gagné, 1974.) In Chapter 3 we alluded to psychological principles that influence educational practice. In this section we refer more specifically to the kind of research that frequently takes place in university laboratories or in laboratory rooms set up in schools.

Psychological research of this kind may be misunderstood by teachers and the communities they serve, and is often discounted by them as an irrelevant activity primarily concerned with providing researchers with academic publications and research students with Ph.D. dissertations. On the other side, researchers often point their fingers at practitioners and laymen for not understanding the ways in which scientific progress occurs.

In many areas of social research (e.g., economic policy, medical research, the dynamics of pollution, the nature of intelligence, and cultural influences on learning), there is heated debate concerning the appropriate, ethical forms of experimentation in which the subjects are human beings. A major factor that can contribute to alleviating the concerns of those involved is maximal two-way, open communication. Researchers need to explain in understandable terms the research they undertake with school children and the code of ethics under which they operate. Teachers and school administrators need to understand how research activity can contribute to the eventual improvement of educational practice. The children involved should also feel that they are contributing members in an overall effort to increase understanding of how we learn, think, and solve problems.

Knowledge and theory accumulate through incremental, painstaking steps. For this work, behavioral scientists require the cooperation of practitioners and laymen because without access to real-world phenomena their sciences can become involuted, sterile, and of little consequence to the larger society. In this section, we give examples of psychological research relating to instruction; we consider such fundamental areas as the competence to be learned and the initial capabilities with which learning begins.

What Is To Be Learned: The Analysis of Competent Performance

Central to understanding instructional processes is the specification and analysis of what it is that is to be learned. What have competent performers in a subject-matter domain learned that distinguishes them from novices? For example, what distinguishes a skilled reader from an unskilled one? What distinguishes someone who has a good working knowledge of geometry from one who does not? The concepts and conceptual relationships used by experts are generally not in the best form for facilitating instruction and the acquisition of competence, and they need to be analyzed and transformed into terms comprehensible to younger or less experienced individuals. An understanding of the difference between levels of competence is required.

The instructional task is to proceed from the initial competence of the learner to advanced competence, and therefore an understanding of the nature of initial, intermediate, and advanced levels provides a guide as to how instruction and learning can best proceed. This problem has been attacked in several ways, which will now be described.

Learning hierarchies. Research has been carried out on the structure of the intellectual skills that are frequently the subject of instruction in elementary schools. A cumulative transfer theory of learning, developed by Gagné (1968, 1970), has been applied to progressions of competence within subject-matter topics that make up particular curricula. Techniques have been developed for specifying sequences of learning achievements in which each learned performance is viewed as a prerequisite for the next level of intellectual performance. As illustrated in Chapter 5, superordinate-subordinate relations recur throughout this progression.

In general, a superordinate or higher-order capability is more readily learned if the subordinate or lower-order capability has been previously learned. The defining characteristic of a subordinate capability is that it has been identified as contributing positive transfer to (i.e., facilitating) the learning of the higher-order capability. As Gagné (1970) wrote:

The theoretically predicted consequence of a subordinate skill that has been previously mastered is that it will facilitate the learning of the higher-level skill to which it is related. In contrast, if the subordinate skill has not been previously mastered, there will be no facilitation of the learning of the higher-level skill. This latter condition does not mean that the higher-level skill cannot be learned—only that, on the average, in the group of students for whom a topic sequence has been designed, learning will not be accomplished readily. . . . there may be two or three subordinate skills that contribute positive transfer to a higher-level skill. Or a single subordinate skill may facilitate the learning of more than one higher-level skill. (pp. 239–240)

Once a learning hierarchy is developed, it can be empirically tested by research with an appropriate group of students to determine whether the hypothesized transfer relations hold. Further examination of the examples of learning hierarchies in beginning arithmetic concepts (see Chapter 5; Figures 5.3, 5.4, and 5.5) should make this notion clear. Other examples in topics such as science and algebra can be found in Gagné (1970), and in Gagné and Briggs (1974).

Learning hierarchies are primarily concerned with the learning of intellectual skills and not with the learning of informational content. Learning hierarchies describe what individuals should be able to do if they are to readily acquire more complex abilities. Learning hierarchies do not directly represent how an individual acquires a store of informational knowledge. For example, when the outcome of instruction is learning verbal information such as the geography of a particular region or the political events that characterize a period in history, then the kind of sequencing described above in the learning of intellectual skills appears to be of less importance; in certain subject matters, for example, learning one fact or set of facts may not make another fact or set of facts more readily learnable. For subject matter that can be analyzed into sequentially learned components, however, learning hierarchies provide a good foundation on which to base curriculum design and instructional practice.

A learning hierarchy can be viewed as a map for guiding the instructional process for individual students and for placing students with respect to their individual level of competence.

Each sequential objective can define a test exercise that an individual passes or fails. "Passing" implies that an individual should be tested on the next superordinate objective; "failing" implies that the student should be tested on subordinate objectives in order to determine whether lack of competence is a result of inadequate performance on prerequisites or inadequate instructions on the new objective.

Learning hierarchies should be used only as guides. A bright student, for example, need not necessarily go through every subordinate skill in a hierarchy; he or she may already know some of the subordinate skills that other students have not learned. A student who is a fast learner may be able to skip over particular steps in a hierarchy because he or she is able to acquire several steps or a group of skills all at once. Other students may require the more step-by-step structure of learning. However, as indicated in Chapter 5, when used appropriately, validated learning hierarchies can provide a basis for guiding the learning routes of different students.

At the present time, both practical and theoretical work is going on to investigate further the nature of learning hierarchies. Their relationships to learning theory and their use for the design of curriculum sequences are being carefully examined (e. g., Resnick, Wang, & Kaplan, 1973; R. T. White, 1973). Questions are being asked about the most effective procedures for teaching the skills in a hierarchy. For example, can lower-order capabilities be taught as heuristics on the basis of which students can discover or invent procedures for carrying out more complex tasks? What is the level of detail to which a hierarchy needs to be specified in order to be generally effective in facilitating learning in a diverse group of students? What are the effects of individual differences on the way students go through the learning of a hierarchy of capabilities? As research attempts to answer these questions, the concept of learning hierarchies is being utilized by educators to build curricula (cf. Gagné & Briggs, 1974).

Process analysis of tasks. Research now being carried out attempts to analyze school tasks in terms of the demands that these tasks place on the child's memory, perceptual abilities, and capabilities for new learning. If the cognitive processes that underlie these task demands can be identified, information might be provided that can be used as a basis for assisting a child in his or her learning. In this section, we describe such research in reading and elementary arithmetic.

In the teaching of *beginning reading*, a pervasive stumbling block is the problem of "blending." After a child has learned to associate letter symbols and sounds (graphemes and phonemes), a significant problem for the child is putting sounds together to make a word. The following kind of behavior is typical (Beck & Mitroff, 1972): A child has learned the sounds for hard *c*, short *a*, and *t*; he or she then encounters for the first time the combination *cat* and reads, "/kuh/ /ah/ /tuh/; *kitten*." This child has learned letter-sound correspondences and has also learned that meaningful units emerge when sounds are put together, but has not learned how to put sounds together.

Traditional reading programs based on phonics have been successful in teaching symbol-sound correspondences to many children; however, they have been less successful in teaching children how to put sounds together. Generally, published teachers' manuals essentially tell the teacher to say something like: "Slide the sounds together." For many children, this is inadequate instruction, and a more specific teaching procedure is required.

Research has been brought to bear on this problem through a combination of practical tryout in the schools and analysis of task processes based upon information processing theory in psychology (Resnick & Beck, 1976). Two blending procedures were examined and analyzed—a "final blending" procedure and a "successive blending" procedure. The general information-processing structures of the two blending routines are shown in Figure 6.2. The routines shown describe how decoding might be carried out for single syllable, regularly spelled words—the typical vocabulary of a beginning phonics program. In (1a) of Figure 6.2, the final blending procedure is depicted. It is called a "final blending" procedure because blending is postponed until the very last step. The sound of each grapheme (letter pattern) is given and stored in memory, and the synthesis or blending occurs after the final phoneme or sound has been pronounced. The child who uses this routine proceeds as follows: "/k/ /a/ /t/ /s/ *cats*." In (1b) of Figure 6.2, the successive blending procedure is depicted; as soon as two sounds are produced, they are blended, and successive phonemes are added to the blend as

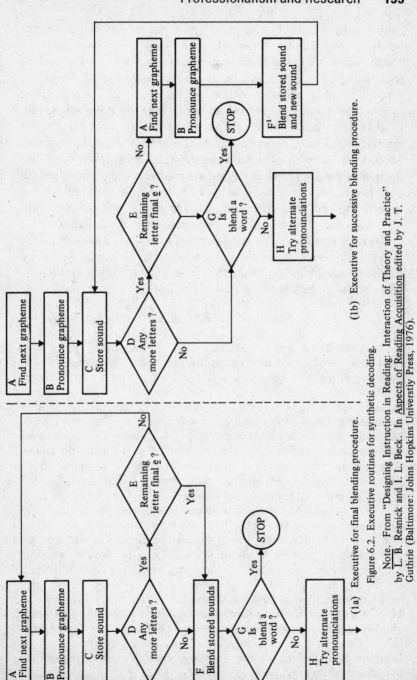

Figure 6.2.   Executive routines for synthetic decoding.

(1a)   Executive for final blending procedure.

(1b)   Executive for successive blending procedure.

Note.   From "Designing Instruction in Reading: Interaction of Theory and Practice"
by L. B. Resnick and I. L. Beck. In Aspects of Reading Acquisition edited by J. T.
Guthrie (Baltimore: Johns Hopkins Universtiy Press, 1976).

they are pronounced. The child using successive blending proceeds in the following fashion: "/k/ /a/ /ka/ /t/ /kat/ /s/ /kats/ *cats*." The lettered components of the two blending routines in Figure 6.2 call upon similar actions and decisions: finding graphemes in sequence A; pronouncing the identified graphemes (sounds), B; remembering the pronounced sound, C; deciding whether more graphemes remain to be sounded, D and E; blending, F; and matching the produced "word" against one's knowledge to determine whether an acceptable word has been produced, G and H. The two routines differ, however, in the way in which the actions and decisions (A through H) are organized, and this organizational difference appears to influence the ease of learning and performing the decoding act.

Resnick and Beck (1976) described how their analyses of the two procedures suggest that the successive blending procedure might be easier for children than the final blending procedure. They wrote as follows:

According to the final blending routine, each grapheme's sound is given, and the full set of phonemes in the word must be held in memory until the entire word has been "sounded out"; only then does any blending occur. But in the successive blending routine, blending occurs sequentially at each stage at which a new phoneme is pronounced. At no time must more than two sounds be held in memory (the sound immediately produced and the one that directly precedes it); and at no time must more than two sound units be blended. Thus, the routines differ in two respects: (1) in the maximum number of sound units to be held in memory during the course of decoding, and (2) in the maximum number of units to be blended during a given attempt. The standard routine on the left [1a of Figure 6.2] requires remembering each of the separate units that the reader identifies as graphemes. The routine on the right [1b] never requires remembering more than two units.

It would seem, at first glance, that while the two routines might produce very different levels of difficulty for the pronunciation of long or complex words, they would be approximately equally difficult for the pronunciation of shorter words (words of no more than three or four graphemes), which compose the beginning reading vocabulary of any phonically oriented instruction. After all, first-grade children normally have a memory span that can easily encompass three elements (as shown, for example, by the digit-span test of the Stanford-Binet, which expects memory of three digits at age three; five at age seven).

Tests such as the digit span, however, require only that items be held in memory. Items need not be generated, and no competing processing interferes with retention. This, however, is not the case during decoding. A substantial amount of other processing must occur simultaneously with the retention of the phoneme elements. Assuming a limited working space or "working memory" (as is common in virtually all current information processing theories), this additional processing is likely to interfere with [other processing]. (pp. 185–186)

Thus, given the fact that memory capacity is limited, especially in young children, the procedure requiring less memory work (the successive blending procedure) should facilitate the decoding process.

Consider another example—research in *elementary arithmetic* on the nature of competent performance in simple addition and subtraction. Several studies (Resnick, 1976; Suppes & Groen, 1967; Woods, Resnick, & Groen, 1975) suggest an interesting relationship between what children are taught to do and how they eventually perform efficiently.

Young children are generally taught to solve a single-digit addition problem such as *6 + 8* by an algorithm in which they count out six blocks, then count eight blocks, and then count to combine the set. With practice, children perform this smoothly; when the blocks are taken away, they frequently shift to counting on their fingers, and then eventually shift to internal processing. When the nature of this internal processing is examined, it is found that most children carry out addition by using what has been called a "choice model." They appear to set a mental counter to the magnitude of whichever number is larger and then increment by the smaller number. It is also found, however, that some children retain the earlier model used in instruction—they increment six times, then increment eight more times, and then read their mental counter.

Unlike these latter children, the more efficient children appear to be able, without direct instruction, to convert a routine that has been taught into a different routine—a routine that shows they have discovered commutativity and have developed a procedure that requires fewer steps. It is to be noted that the initial teaching procedure reflected the rational "union of sets" definition of addition, and thus is a mathematically correct procedure that represents the subject matter clearly and provides a routine that is easy to demonstrate and learn. For an efficient performer, however, the routine is awkward and slow. Thus, the routine derived by rational analysis of the subject-matter structure is transformed to a performance routine that reflects a more sophisticated definition of the subject matter.

What are the implications of this analysis? On the face of it, it would seem that we ought to abandon the algorithm suggested by direct analysis of tasks in favor of analysis of skilled performance. We can argue that the rational analysis of tasks may not match skilled performance and that it therefore should not be used as a basis for instruction. It would seem best to carry out detailed empirical analyses of skilled performance on subject-matter tasks and teach the routines uncovered by such analyses.

However, in discussing this work, Resnick (1976) pointed out that such a conclusion could be in error, since it rests on the assumption that efficient instruction is necessarily direct instruction in skilled performance strategies rather than instruction in routines that put learners in a good position to invent or derive efficient strategies for themselves. So, it is implied that the teaching routines in elementary arithmetic were not poor ones that inhibited the acquisition of efficient performance, but may have been good ones that fostered the invention of more efficient algorithms. It is also implied that it would be desirable to develop instructional routines to teach the more efficient procedure directly to students who do not discover it on their own.

Where Learning Begins: Cognitive Strategies and Readiness Skills

Closely allied to the problem of describing what is to be learned is the problem of describing the capabilities of learners as they begin instruction. Instruction begins with these "initial state" capabilities and proceeds from this base toward the development of competent performance. These initial capabilities are generally called readiness skills, aptitudes, and learning styles, and they include knowledge and styles of thinking picked up from one's experiences with one's family and others, or from prior educational experiences.

Describing entering capabilities is a critical step in making school programs adaptive to individual differences. In order to begin instruction, it is necessary to know what the individual learner can and cannot do relevant to the subject matter to be learned and what generalized learning-to-learn skills he or she has. For effective instruction, characterization and diagnosis of the entering capabilities of the learner must be made in terms relevant to educational decision making, that is, to the next instructional steps that can be undertaken.

As indicated in previous chapters, global classificatory labels such as high or low IQ, learning disabled, or high or low aptitude are not as useful for the purposes of individualizing instruction as are descriptions of specific competencies that can be observed in particular learning situations. These specific competencies can then be related to the kinds of instructional procedures most likely to be effective with the children involved.

Describing the capabilities of the learner for the purposes of adaptive instruction is not done only at the outset of instruction, similar to aptitude and intelligence tests given only at the beginning of a period of schooling; rather, a more continuous process is required. Changes in both specific knowledge and skill and in generalized cognitive abilities result from experiences outside formal instruction as well as from engaging in the instruction itself. Thus, to maintain an effectively adaptive curriculum over an extended period of time, it is necessary to describe changes in the learner's capabilities as instruction progresses and to consider this updated description of entering capabilities in making decisions as to the course of succeeding instruction. Teachers and students need to be in a position to obtain and utilize this kind of information. With it, teachers can prescribe instruction, and students can assess their own abilities and learning,and select appropriate instruction.

Some basic readiness skills. In the primary grades, a frequent concern is the extent to which children have certain fundamental capabilities that contribute to their success in learning. An interesting example of research in this area was that carried out by Rosner (1972), which led to the development of the Perceptual Skills Curriculum described in Chapter 5. The problem Rosner attacked was the identification of basic visual and auditory skills of young children that are prerequisite to their ability to learn to read and to learn basic number concepts in arithmetic. Many children do not gain proper facility with these fundamental readiness processes, and are drawn into a cycle of cumulating deficit and increasing difficulty in learning the fundamental literacies.

Over several years, Rosner's program of research proceeded through a number of stages from research and development to tested school use. The first stage had as its objective the identification of auditory and visual perceptual skills that might be directly related to basic classroom tasks in beginning reading and arithmetic (see Chapter 3). On the basis of previous research on the development of visual- and auditory-motor skills in children, a battery of tests was devised to probe what appeared to be critical perceptual skills. Particularly emphasized (as described in Chapter 5) were: (a) the ability to analyze a spoken word into its component sound parts, a kind of acoustical processing that is a prerequisite readiness proficiency for the tasks of beginning reading; and (b) the perception of spatial groupings and arrangements of objects that is basic to mapping these arrangements with numerical symbols indicating quantity.

The tests were administered to a broad sample of preschool, kindergarten, and primary-grade children, and this same sample was tested at a later date with standardized tests of academic achievement in beginning reading and elementary arithmetic concepts. Through correlational analysis techniques, a search was made for significant relationships between the various perceptual tests and achievement test scores. Once preliminary evidence was obtained of significant relationships between specific perceptual skills and certain achievement subtest scores, the perceptual skills involved were further analyzed through laboratory experimentation into relevant dimensions of perceptual skill readiness that could be related to school learning procedures.

The task of the second stage of the project was to determine whether the identified readiness skills could be effectively taught through appropriate instructional procedures. The question was: Could such perceptual skills be trained, or are they largely dependent upon the way in which a child grows and develops? How modifiable are these fundamental skills? The outcome of a series of studies with children at the ages of three, four, and five provided evidence that the auditory-motor and visual-motor skills could be influenced by instruction. The effects of this instruction were not just rote learning, but were transferable to situations not identical to those used in training.

Given the identification of instructible perceptual skills that were relevant to classroom achievement, the objective of the third stage of the project was to determine whether the effect of this instruction was strong enough to be apparent and measurable in classroom achievement. Studies carried out along these lines showed differences on standardized achievement tests between children who were instructed and those who were not.

The work of the fourth stage of the project, given the evidence of the three previous stages, was to describe and package the instructional program in a way that allowed it to be implemented in classrooms. In this stage, a preliminary experimental form of a perceptual, motor curriculum was developed and further tested in classroom settings to assess its effectiveness and improve its design. Following this work, the curriculum was released for general use. Representative samples of the sequenced objectives of the visual-motor component and the auditory-motor component of the Perceptual Skills Curriculum are presented in Chapter 5 in Tables 5.3 and 5.4, respectively.

The processes of intelligence and aptitude. Chapter 3 pointed out how new work in cognitive psychology and in the individualization of instruction raises the question of the extent to which aptitude-like behavior is subject to educational influence. Also mentioned was that the teaching of basic cognitive abilities such as perceptual skills, memory organization skills, problem-solving skills, and learning-to-learn skills could become an expressed part of the curriculum. In essence, this implies that what is taught in school could include the processes of intelligence and aptitude.

If research brings about an understanding of these processes, then we can influence learning in two ways: (a) by designing instructional alternatives that adapt to these processes, and (b) by attempting to improve an individual's competence in these processes so that he or she is more likely to profit from the available instructional procedures. Research along these lines is at this time only tentative and suggestive; but the field is developing rapidly, and we present some interesting examples here of research that may contribute to identifying teachable basic abilities.

A research article by Estes (1974) discussed the *digit-span test of immediate memory* that appears on the Stanford-Binet intelligence test. At the ten-year level, the individual's task is to repeat a sequence of random digits that has been read aloud by the examiner. If the digits are recalled in order, the individual is scored as passing this subtest. The interesting instructional question, however, is: If an individual scores low on this test, what intructional procedure might be useful in improving that performance?

Recent research and theory dealing with short-term memory for sequences of items suggest that, in general, the following kind of cognitive processes are involved (see Johnson, 1970): On presentation of the digit sequence 691472, the individual is conceived to subgroup the sequence into two chunks, each of which is maintained in memory. Within each chunk, the items of the sequence are assigned the ordinal members 1, 2, and 3. When asked to recall the string of digits, the individual brings into memory each of the two chunks with their associated ordinal positions. While this process goes on, the individual holds the partially reconstructed sequence in memory and constructs the next chunk until reconstruction of the entire string is complete.

Such a theoretical analysis of performance of the digit-span task has possible implications for assessing differences in the kind of cognitive competence individuals bring to this task. Young children or children who are regarded as poor learners might fail this test because they have insufficient familiarity with the ordinal number sequence (i.e., with counting) or because of inexperience in ordering materials using the number sequence. It is possible that an individual has not developed an appropriate grouping strategy and is unable to take advantage of chunking to relieve the burden on memory. Or, perhaps the individual has difficulty in holding part of the digit sequence in memory while organizing the entire sequence. If the source of difficulty in these hypothesized processes could be localized, then it might be of considerable help in indicating how deficient processes can be remedied through instruction.

The series of studies by Hunt, Frost, and Lunneborg (1973), reported in Chapter 3, are relevant here. In these studies, *the characteristics of high-verbal ability and high-quantitative ability* students, as defined by aptitude tests, were examined in terms of tasks that tapped cognitive processes. The conclusions from the studies indicated a relationship between verbal ability and the rapidity and efficiency of manipulating information in short-term memory, and between quantitative ability and resistance to distraction while consolidating information in short-term memory. If this work proves to be substantiated as more evidence is obtained, and if further situations are identified where the speed and other properties of memory processing are shown to be predictive of school achievement, then clues might be available as to how the processes that underlie verbal and mathematical aptitude might be modified by or employed for learning.

Another study (Holzman, Glaser, & Pellegrino, 1976) investigated *letter series completion problems* of the kind used in tests of intelligence. Letter series consist of a sequence of alphabetic characters running in a consistent pattern. For example, the individual might see the problem "defgefghfghi __ __ __ __" and be asked to fill in the blanks. The individual must fill in the four blanks with letters that are consistent with the pattern exhibited by the previously presented letters of that series. Theoretical and experimental studies (Kotovsky & Simon, 1973; Simon & Kotovsky, 1963) have suggested that four basic component routines are necessary for obtaining a correct solution.

The first routine is the detection of *relations* between letters. Are letters identical, sequential, or sequential in reverse order? The second routine or subskill is the discovery of *periodicity* in a series. This involves noticing that letter relations repeat themselves at regular, predictable intervals. A third routine, called *pattern description*, assembles knowledge of letter relations and knowledge of periodicity into a rule that generates the series. The final routine required is *extrapolation*. This involves remembering the pattern description and using this rule to generate the appropriate letters for the blanks.

Using this information about possible cognitive processes involved, Holzman and his colleagues taught elementary school children to be very proficient in the detection of relations and the discovery of periodicity. As a result of their training, children were able to show substantial pretest to posttest gains on a typical letter-series completion test. Most strikingly, the children were significantly more able than uninstructed individuals to demonstrate perfect posttest solutions to the types of problems they found difficult on the pretest. Although both the uninstructed children (as a result of repeated testing) and instructed children were able to make gains on easy problems, the children trained on component subskills seemed to have acquired an information management strategy that allowed them frequently to reach perfect solution even on difficult problems. While the skills taught to the children in this study were quite specific, the question is raised about the possibilities for the analysis of more general abilities that might provide a basis for truly generative intellectual abilities.

Studies such as the three described suggest that research on the cognitive processes that underlie intelligence and aptitude-like performance may provide information that can increase the likelihood of the success of children in school. It is hoped that this kind of research will lead to diagnostic measuring instruments that will provide information about how individuals can be instructed in a way that improves their abilities to learn and to profit from instruction.

Learning-to-learn skills. A significant aspect of cognitive skill is the efficiency with which learning occurs under conditions with little formal instruction. In fact, virtually all the learning that children manage prior to school entrance occurs without formal instruction. During the school years, much of what is learned is not a part of any formal curriculum, and during most of one's adult life, there is little formal instruction; and yet, learning certainly continues. Even where deliberate instruction is provided, it is rarely "complete" in terms of assuring that the learner experiences or attends to every aspect of what is to be learned, or that he or she is systematically taught every skill in the form used by highly competent individuals.

The foregoing observations suggest that an important aspect of an individual's cognitive ability is that of acquiring new competencies under conditions of limited or less than explicit instruction. Thus, an appropriate concern for instruction is the teaching of general strategies that will help individuals learn on their own. An interest in teaching such general "learning-to-learn" abilities has been widely expressed by educators, but at the present time there is little psychological basis for such instruction. One possible basis can come from the studies of the processes underlying the aptitude-like skills just described. Still another potential basis for such instruction might be deduced from theoretical and experimental analyses of how people solve problems.

Recent research (Resnick & Glaser, 1976) suggests that the processes involved in certain kinds of problem solving are probably similar to the processes involved in learning in the absence of direct or complete instruction, and that instruction in these processes might constitute a means of increasing an individual's generalized learning-to-learn ability. An analysis of certain problem-solving tasks shows that three phases are involved: (a) problem detection, in which the inapplicability of usual procedures for solving a problem is noted and a problem is formulated; (b) feature detection, in which the task environment is scanned for cues that might lead to appropriate actions for solution; and (c) goal analysis, in which subgoals are successively reformulated on the basis of cues from the environment in order to yield partial solutions that contribute eventually to solution of the total problem.

A study by Schadler and Pellegrino (1974) has shown that requiring children to verbalize (i.e., to speak aloud) their goals and strategies in each of these phases before they make actual moves toward solution greatly increases the likelihood of problem solution. Along these lines, it seems reasonable to suggest that ways might be found to make individuals more conscious of their problem-solving techniques. Individuals might also be taught strategies for identifying the features of a task that will enhance the possibility of noticing cues that prompt effective action and of avoiding cues that lead to ineffective actions. Such self-regulation could be a major characteristic of successful self-learning and problem solving. In the future, research may be able to offer suggestions for the instruction of such generalized learning-to-learn abilities.

Summary

In this chapter we have argued for the continued professionalization of teaching through increasing involvement and partnership in research and development. We have described a number of areas where this is taking place: directly with respect to research on classroom practices and the effects of instruction, and the development and testing of new curriculum materials and procedures; and less directly with respect to the study of cognitive processes that are involved in the performance of school tasks and on the abilities that students bring to them. The areas described in this chapter represent selections of special interest to the author, and they far from exhaust the important kind of work that needs to be done, or the various scholarly and scientific disciplines that must consider instruction and education as a subject matter for study.

Most importantly, we mean to call attention to the interaction between practice, development, implementation, and research whereby an experimental mood in education is created and preserved. This attitude should encourage the idea of an "experimenting society" (Campbell, 1971) in which school administrators, teachers, students, parents, curriculum designers, and scientists have a direct part to play in improving their schools. As has been well described by Campbell, an experimenting society is one that vigorously tries out proposed solutions to recurrent problems, makes hardheaded and multidimensional evaluations of outcomes, and moves on to try alternatives when evaluations show a reform to have been ineffective. An experimenting society encourages exploratory innovation and is committed to research as a basis for action. Experimental endeavors should challenge the status quo and provide for informed change by supplying reasonable alternatives for the community to consider and from which to choose.

References

Anderson, S. B., Bogatz, G. A., Draper, T. W., Jungeblut, A., Sidwell, G., Ward, W. C., & Yates, A. *CIRCUS—Manual and technical report* (preliminary edition). Princeton, N.J.: Educational Testing Service, 1974–75.

Angoff, W. H. (Ed.). *The College Board Admissions Testing Program: A technical report on research and development activities relating to the Scholastic Aptitude Test and Achievement Tests.* New York: College Entrance Examination Board, 1971.

Atkinson, R. C. Teaching children to read using a computer. *American Psychologist,* 1974, *29,* 169–178.

Atkinson, R. C., & Hansen, D. N. Computer-assisted instruction in initial reading: The Stanford project. *Reading Research Quarterly,* 1966, *2,* 5–25.

Atkinson, R. C., & Wilson, H. A. (Eds.). *Computer-assisted instruction: A book of readings.* New York: Academic Press, 1969.

Beck, I. I. Comprehension during the acquisition of decoding skills. In J. T. Guthrie (Ed.), *Cognition, curriculum and comprehension.* Newark, Del.: International Reading Association, in press.

Beck, I. L., & Mitroff, D. D. *The rationale and design of a primary grades reading system for an individualized classroom.* Pittsburgh: University of Pittsburgh, Learning Research and Development Center, 1972.

Benjamin, H. *The cultivation of idiosyncrasy.* Cambridge, Mass.: Harvard University Press, 1949.

Bonn, M. An American paradox. *American Education,* 1974, *10,* 24–28.

Bransford, J. D., & Franks, J. J. The abstraction of linguistic ideas. *Cognitive Psychology,* 1971, *2,* 331–350.

Brooks, H. Physics and the polity. *Science,* 1968, *160,* 396–400.

Broudy, H. S. *The real world of the public schools.* New York: Harcourt Brace Jovanovich, 1972.

Burt, C., Jones, E., Miller, E., & Moodie, W. *How the mind works.* New York: Appleton-Century-Crofts, 1934.

Campbell, D. T. *Methods for the experimenting society.* Paper presented at the annual meeting of the American Psychological Association, Washington, D.C., September 1971.

Champagne, A. B., & Klopfer, L. E. An individualized elementary school science program. *Theory into Practice,* 1974, *13,* 136–148.

Champagne, A. B., & Klopfer, L. E. *Level E teacher's manual, individualized science.* Kankakee, Ill.: Imperial International Learning Corp., 1975.

Cole, M., Gay, J., Glick, J. A., & Sharp, D. W. *The cultural context of learning and thinking: An exploration in experimental anthropology.* New York: Basic Books, 1971.

Coleman, J. S. Equality of opportunity and equality of results. *Harvard Educational Review,* 1973, *43,* 129–137.

Coleman, J. S., Campbell, E. Q., Hobson, C. J., McPartland, J., Mood, A. M., Weinfeld, F. D., & York, R. L. *Equality of educational opportunity.* Washington, D.C.: U.S. Government Printing Office, 1966.

Cooley, W. W., & Emrick, J. A. *A model of classroom differences which explains variation in classroom achievement.* Paper presented at the annual meeting of the American Educational Research Association, Chicago, April 1974.

Cooley, W. W., & Glaser, R. The computer and individualized instruction. *Science,* 1969, *166,* 574–582.

Cooley, W. W., & Leinhardt, G. *The application of a model for investigating classroom processes.* Pittsburgh: University of Pittsburgh, Learning Research and Development Center, 1975.

Cooley, W. W., & Lohnes, P. R. *Evaluation research in education.* New York: Irvington Publishers, 1976.

Cremin, L. A. *The transformation of the school.* New York: Vintage Books, 1961.

Cronbach, L. J. How can instruction be adapted to individual differences? In R. M. Gagné (Ed.), *Learning and individual differences.* Columbus, Ohio: Charles E. Merrill, 1967.

Cronbach, L. J. Five decades of public controversy over mental testing. *American Psychologist,* 1975, *30,* 1–14.

Cross, K. P. *Beyond the open door.* San Francisco: Jossey-Bass, 1971.

David, E. E., Jr. The relation of science and technology. *Science,* 1972, *175,* 13.

Day, M. C., & Parker, R. K. *The preschool in action: Exploring early childhood programs* (2nd ed.). Boston: Allyn & Bacon, 1976.

Dewey, J. Psychology and social practice. *The Psychological Review*, 1900, 7, 105–124.

Dewey, J. The child and the curriculum. In R. D. Archambault (Ed.), *John Dewey on education: Selected writings*. New York: The Modern Library, 1964. (Originally published, 1902)

Dewey, J. *Experience and education*. New York: Collier Books, 1973. (Originally published, 1938)

Dobzhansky, T. *Genetic diversity and human equality*. New York: Basic Books, 1973.

Downey, M. T. *Ben D. Wood: Educational reformer*. Princeton, N.J.: Educational Testing Service, 1965.

Ebbinghaus, H. [*Memory*] (H. A. Ruger & C. E. Bussenius, trans.). New York: Dover, 1964. (Originally published, 1885)

Estes, W. K. Learning theory and intelligence. *American Psychologist*, 1974, 29, 740–749.

Gagné, R. M. The acquisition of knowledge. *Psychological Review*, 1962, 69, 355–365.

Gagné, R. M. Learning hierarchies. *Educational Psychologist*, 1968, 6, 1–9.

Gagné, R. M. *The conditions of learning* (2nd ed.). New York: Holt, Rinehart and Winston, 1970.

Gagné, R. M. *Essentials of learning for instruction*. Hinsdale, Ill.: Dryden Press, 1974.

Gagné, R. M., & Briggs, L. J. *Principles of instructional design*. New York: Holt, Rinehart and Winston, 1974.

Gardner, J. W. *Excellence: Can we be equal and excellent too?* New York: Harper & Row, 1961.

Gesell, A. *The embryology of behavior: The beginnings of the human mind*. New York: Harper & Row, 1945.

Gesell, A. The ontogenesis of infant behavior. In L. Carmichael (Ed.), *Manual of child psychology*. New York: Wiley, 1946.

Gibson, E. J., & Levin, H. *The psychology of reading*. Cambridge, Mass: M.I.T. Press, 1975.

Glaser, R. Adapting the elementary school curriculum to individual performance. In *Proceedings of the 1967 Invitational Conference on Testing Problems*. Princeton, N.J.: Educational Testing Service, 1968.

Glaser, R. Individuals and learning: The new aptitudes. *Educational Researcher*, 1972, 1, 5–13.

Glaser, R. The processes of intelligence and education. In L. B.

Resnick (Ed.), *The nature of intelligence*. Hillsdale, N.J.: Lawrence Erlbaum Asssociates, 1976.

Glaser, R., & Resnick, L. B. Instructional psychology. *Annual Review of Psychology*, 1972, *23*, 207–276.

Gow, D. T. *Design and development of curricular materials*. Pittsburgh: University of Pittsburgh, Center for International Studies, 1976.

Henry, N. B. (Ed.). *Learning and instruction* (Forty-ninth Yearbook of the National Society for the Study of Education, Pt. 1). Chicago: NSSE, 1950.

Hilgard, E. R. (Ed.). *Theories of learning and instruction* (Sixty-third Yearbook of the National Society for the Study of Education, Pt. 1). Chicago: NSSE, 1964.

Holland, J. G., Solomon, C., Doran, J., & Frezza, D. A. *The analysis of behavior in planning instruction*. Reading, Mass.: Addison-Wesley, 1976.

Holzman, T. G., Glaser, R., & Pellegrino, J. W. Process training derived from a computer simulation theory. *Memory & Cognition*, 1976, *4*, 349–356.

Hunt, E., Frost, N., & Lunneborg, C. Individual differences in cognition: A new approach to intelligence. In G. H. Bower (Ed.), *The psychology of learning and motivation* (Vol. 7). New York: Academic Press, 1973.

Hunt, E., Lunneborg, C., & Lewis, J. What does it mean to be high verbal? *Cognitive Psychology*, 1975, *7*, 194–227.

Hunt, J. McV. *Intelligence and experience*. New York: Ronald Press, 1961.

Jackson, P. W., Rivlin, A. M., Edmonds, R. Michelson, S., Thurow, L. C., Clark, K. B., Duncan, B., Coleman, J. S., & Jencks, C. Perspectives on *Inequality*: A reassessment of the effect of fam ily and schooling in America. *Harvard Educational Review*, 1973, *43*, 37–164.

Jencks, C., Smith, M., Acland, H., Bane, M. J., Cohen, D., Gintis, H., Heyns, B., & Michelson, S. *Inequality: A reassessment of the effect of family and schooling in America*. New York: Basic Books, 1972.

Johnson, N. F. The role of chunking and organization in the process of recall. In G. H. Bower (Ed.), *The psychology of learning and motivation* (Vol. 4). New York: Academic Press, 1970.

Keller, F. S. "Good-bye, teacher . . ." *Journal of Applied Behavior Analysis*, 1968, *1*, 79–89.

Klopfer, L. E. Individualized science: Relevance for the 1970's. *Science Education*, 1971, *55*, 441–448.

Kohlberg, L. Early education: A cognitive-developmental view. *Child Development*, 1968, *39*, 1013–1062.

Kotovsky, K., & Simon, H. A. Empirical tests of a theory of human acquisition of concepts for sequential patterns. *Cognitive Psychology*, 1973, *4*, 399–424.

Leinhardt, G. *Development and tryout of the Adaptive Teacher Skills Instrument.* Unpublished manuscript, University of Pittsburgh, Learning Research and Development Center, 1975.

Lindsay, P. H., & Norman, D. A. *Human information processing: An introduction to psychology.* New York: Academic Press, 1972.

Lindvall, C. M., & Bolvin, J. O. Programed instruction in the schools: An application of programing principles in "Individually Prescribed Instruction." In P. C. Lange (Ed.), *Programed instruction* (Sixty-sixth Yearbook of the National Society for the Study of Education, Pt. 2). Chicago: NSSE, 1967.

Lockard, R. B. Reflections on the fall of comparative psychology: Is there a message for us all? *American Psychologist*, 1971, *26*, 168–179.

McClearn, G. E. Genes and development. In M. Manosevitz, G. Lindzey, & D. D. Thiessen (Eds.), *Behavioral genetics: Method and research.* New York: Appleton-Century-Crofts, 1969.

McClelland, D. C. Encouraging excellence: The stranglehold of academic performance on the admissions process. *Harvard Alumni Bulletin,* November, 1961, pp. 161–165.

McNemar, Q. Lost: Our intelligence? Why? *American Psychologist*, 1964, *19*, 871–882.

Mayeske, G. W., Wisler, C. E., Beaton, A. E., Jr., Weinfeld, F. D., Cohen, W. M., Okada, T., Proshek, J. M., & Tabler, K. A. *A study of our nation's schools.* Washington, D.C.: U.S. Government Printing Office, 1972. (Originally published, 1969.)

Merrill, M. D. (Ed.). *Instructional design: Readings.* Englewood Cliffs, N.J.: Prentice-Hall, 1971.

Mischel, W. Toward a cognitive social learning reconceptualization of personality. *Psychological Review,* 1973, *80*, 252–283.

Panel on Youth of the President's Science Advisory Committee. *Youth: Transition to adulthood.* Chicago: University of Chicago Press, 1974.

Popham, W. J., & Baker, E. L. *Establishing instructional goals.* Englewood Cliffs, N.J.: Prentice-Hall, 1970. (a)

Popham, W. J., & Baker, E. L. *Planning an instructional sequence.* Englewood Cliffs, N.J.: Prentice-Hall, 1970. (b)

Popham, W. J., & Baker, E. L. *Systematic instruction.* Englewood Cliffs, N.J.: Prentice-Hall, 1970. (c)

Resnick, L. B. *Design of an early learning curriculum.* Pittsburgh: University of Pittsburgh, Learning Research and Development Center, 1967.

Resnick, L. B. *Open education: Some tasks for technology.* Pittsburgh: University of Pittsburgh, Learning Research and Development Center, 1972.

Resnick, L. B. (Ed.). Hierarchies in children's learning: A symposium. *Instructional Science,* 1973, *2,* 311–362.

Resnick, L. B. The science and art of curriculum design. In J. Schaffarzick & D. H. Hampson (Eds.), *Strategies for curriculum development.* Berkeley, Calif.: McCutchan Publishing Corp., 1975.

Resnick, L. B. Task analysis in instructional design: Some cases from mathematics. In D. Klahr (Ed.), *Cognition and instruction.* Hillsdale, N.J.: Lawrence Erlbaum Associates, 1976.

Resnick, L. B., & Beck, I. L. Designing instruction in reading: Interaction of theory and practice. In J. T. Guthrie (Ed.), *Aspects of reading acquisition.* Baltimore: Johns Hopkins University Press, 1976.

Resnick, L. B., & Glaser, R. Problem solving and intelligence. In L. B. Resnick (Ed.), *The nature of intelligence.* Hillsdale, N.J.: Lawrence Erlbaum Associates, 1976.

Resnick, L. B., Wang, M. C., & Kaplan, J. Task analysis in curriculum design: A hierarchically sequenced introductory mathematics curriculum. *Journal of Applied Behavior Analysis,* 1973, *6,* 679–710.

Resnick, L. B., Wang, M. C., & Rosner, J. Adaptive education for young children: The Primary Education Project. In M. C. Day & R. K. Parker (Eds.), *The preschool in action: Exploring early childhood programs* (2nd ed.). Boston: Allyn & Bacon, in press.

Riesen, A. Effects of early deprivation of photic stimulation. In S. F. Osler & R. E. Cooke (Eds.), *The biosocial basis of mental retardation.* Baltimore: Johns Hopkins Press, 1965.

Rivlin, A. M. Forensic social science. *Harvard Educational Review,* 1973, *43,* 61–75.

Rosner, J. *The development and validation of an individualized perceptual skills curriculum.* Pittsburgh: University of Pittsburgh, Learning Research and Development Center, 1972.

Rosner, J. Language arts and arithmetic achievement, and specifically related perceptual skills. *American Educational Research Journal,* 1973, *10,* 59–68. (a)

Rosner, J. *Perceptual skills curriculum* (6 vols.). New York: Walker Educational Book Corp., 1973. (b)

Schadler, M., & Pellegrino, J. W. *Maximizing performance in a problem solving task.* Unpublished manuscript, University of Pittsburgh, Learning Research and Development Center, 1974.

Schudson, M. S. Organizing the "meritocracy": A history of the College Entrance Examination Board. *Harvard Educational Review,* 1972, *42,* 34–69.

Sherman, J. G. (Ed.). *Personalized System of Instruction: 41 germinal papers.* Menlo Park, Calif.: W. A. Benjamin, Inc., 1974.

Simon, H. A., & Kotovsky, K. Human acquisition of concepts for sequential patterns. *Psychological Review,* 1963, *70,* 534–546.

Stallings, J. A., & Kaskowitz, D. H. *Follow through classroom observation evaluation, 1972–1973.* Menlo Park, Calif.: Stanford Research Institute, 1974.

Suppes, P., & Groen, G. Some counting models for first-grade performance data on simple addition facts. In J. M. Scandura (Ed.), *Research in mathematics education.* Washington, D.C.: National Council of Teachers of Mathematics, 1967.

Suppes, P., Jerman, M., & Brian, D. *Computer-assisted instruction: Stanford's 1965–66 arithmetic program.* New York: Academic Press, 1968.

Talmage, H. (Ed.). *Systems of individualized education.* Berkeley, Calif.: McCutchan Publishing Corp., 1975.

Thorndike, E. L. *Individuality.* Boston: Houghton Mifflin, 1911.

Thorndike, E. L. *The psychology of arithmetic.* New York: Macmillan, 1922.

Thorndike, E. L., Cobb, M. V., Orleans, J. S., Symonds, P. M., Wald, E., & Woodyard, E. *The psychology of algebra.* New York: Macmillan, 1923.

Thorndike, R. L., & Hagen, E. *Ten thousand careers.* New York: Wiley, 1959.

Tuddenham, R. D. The nature and measurement of intelligence. In L. Postman (Ed.), *Psychology in the making.* New York: Alfred A. Knopf, 1962.

Tyler, L. E. The intelligence we test—An evolving concept. In L. B. Resnick (Ed.), *The nature of intelligence.* Hillsdale, N.J.: Lawrence Erlbaum Associates, 1976.

Wang, M. C. *Teacher's manual for the exploratory learning component of the classification and communication skills curriculum* (2 vols.). Pittsburgh: University of Pittsburgh, Learning Research and Development Center, 1973. (a)

Wang, M. C. *Teacher's manual for the exploratory learning component of the LRDC individualized instructional program for the early learning grades* (2 vols.). Pittsburgh: University of Pittsburgh, Learning Research and Development Center, 1973. (b)

Wang, M. C. *The rationale and design of the self-schedule system.*

Pittsburgh: University of Pittsburgh, Learning Research and Development Center, 1974.

Washburne, C. W. Introduction and summary. In G. M. Whipple (Ed.), *Adapting the schools to individual differences* (Twenty-fourth Yearbook of the National Society for the Study of Education, Pt. 2). Chicago: NSSE, 1925.

White, B. L. Child development research: An edifice without a foundation. *Merrill-Palmer Quarterly*, 1969, *15*, 49–79.

White, R. T. Research into learning hierarchies. *Review of Educational Research*, 1973, *43*, 361–375.

Wing, C. W., Jr., & Wallach, M. A. *College admissions and the psychology of talent*. New York: Holt, Rinehart and Winston, 1971.

Wolf, T. H. *Alfred Binet*. Chicago: University of Chicago Press, 1973.

Woods, S. S., Resnick, L. B., & Groen, G. J. An experimental test of five process models for subtraction. *Journal of Educational Psychology*, 1975, *67*, 17–21.

Index